THE
DEREK SANDERSON
NOBODY KNOWS

THE DEREK SANDERSON NOBODY KNOWS

At 26 the World's Highest Paid Athlete

Gerald Eskenazi

FOLLETT PUBLISHING COMPANY
Chicago

OTHER BOOKS BY THE AUTHOR

HOCKEY
A YEAR ON ICE
A THINKING MAN'S GUIDE TO PRO HOCKEY
HOCKEY IS MY LIFE (with Phil Esposito)
THE STORY OF HOCKEY

Library of Congress Catalog Card Number: 73-82200

ISBN: 0-695-80424-3

First printing

For Mark Eskenazi, My Favorite Hockey Player

THE
DEREK SANDERSON
NOBODY KNOWS

One

IT WAS a twenty-nine-cent football and Derek Sanderson wanted it.

"No," said his mother to the eight-year-old Derek, a skinny little boy with narrow eyes that were filling with tears. "We can't afford it."

"But I want it," he screamed.

"No."

"I'm funny that way," the man would recall almost twenty years later. "I nagged and pleaded until she said okay. She gave up and she brought the thing home."

And that was the last time Derek Sanderson touched his twenty-nine-cent football.

"It was always like that with me," he explained. "Once I got something I really wanted I lost interest in it. Imagine, a damn twenty-nine-cent football. I made my mother buy it even though it was too expensive and then I couldn't even look at it again."

Sanderson is twenty-six years old, sitting in a lawyer's office with a man named Jim Cooper, the owner of the Philadelphia Blazers of the World Hockey Association. Among the group is Bob Woolf, Sanderson's attorney.

"I think you're going to like what you have to hear, Derek," says Woolf, grinning.

Woolf picks up a thickly folded piece of paper and recites:

"Derek, you will receive $2.65 million to play hockey five years with the Philadelphia Blazers. This year you will be paid more than $500,000 in cash. The rest of the money will be paid to you over the next ten years. You have become the highest paid athlete in the world. How does that sound?"

It is, of course, the most absurd scene in the history of money and those who play for it. Sanderson thinks briefly that finally, it is his, everything he could ask for. He jumps up.

"I don't like it," he blurts out.

"What?" shouts Cooper.

"I don't like it," Derek repeats evenly. "I don't have any friends in Philadelphia."

Cooper stares at him and says, finally, "Derek, for $2.65 million, you can buy all the friends you want."

There is, it appears, this constant gap between the present Derek Sanderson and the boy of the 1950s. At the moment of triumph, at the time any of us would say to ourselves, "At last, it's finally mine," there is a leap back in time.

So it was during that million-dollar meeting. Word filtered out and North American newspapers, television and radio stations, fans, and athletes wondered about it.

Could it be true? Could it possibly be true? Was someone simply blowing smoke?

It was true.

The paper with the dollar signs did exist. Woolf was there, the man who had leaped from relative obscurity in a few years to become the most prominent sports attorney in the world. Cooper, a benign, soft-spoken lawyer-businessman from Atlantic City, was real and ready with the money. Sanderson's closest friends, partners with him in a string of singles bars in Boston named for F. Scott Fitzgerald characters, also were on hand. And, of course, so was Derek.

He looks athletic, and he looks different. It's not so much his strange handsomeness (one imagines the face without the slight scar traces and thinks of a boyish-looking priest), the mustache, or the carefully deranged hair. Or is it even his movement, which reflects more accurately his 170 pounds than it does his six-foot frame. The eyes are the thing. He's laughing behind those eyes, which can slant with a suspicious look or narrow when he's just said something outrageous ("I didn't lose my virginity until I was twenty years old"). Derek Sanderson's eyes give him away. And what do they tell you? Simple: You figure it out.

Everyone laughed when the announcement was made at the John F. Kennedy Plaza in Philadelphia. "They made me an offer I couldn't refuse," said Derek, not quite laughing, still attempting to grasp the meaning of this unheard-of money. Is he stoned because his speech is slurred? Is it one too many of vodka and orange juice ("I don't say screwdriver because that sounds like high school")? No, it's just that for today Derek has become a p.r. man, grasping at a clever phrase of the day, borrowed from *The Godfather*. The

phrase sticks, gets quoted. Then Derek recalls the death-
bed line of W.C. Fields and announces, "On second
thought, I'd rather be in Philadelphia." That's cool, another phrase reporters can hang their hats on. But in
the back of his mind, very carefully plotted, is this one
thing: Don't bad-mouth Boston. Don't knock the Bruins.
And so Derek agrees to jump from the National Hockey
League, from the team that has finished first and taken
the Stanley Cup, to the Blazers of the World Hockey
Association, a first-year league of outcasts, jumpers,
and those who never were.

Joe Namath, Wilt Chamberlain, Pele, Hank Aaron
—move over. You're not number one any more. It is the
summer of '72, and Derek Sanderson (b. Niagara Falls,
Ontario, twenty-six years old) is going to make more
money than any of you dreamed of. You at least had
led your sports in something, handling a sphere with as
much or more talent than anyone had before you. You
men were worth the $200,000 you were getting paid.
But Sanderson? He'd never led the National Hockey
League in anything except shorthanded goals. He's
never been on even the second all-star team.

Yet, he is the man the fans love to hate. In St. Louis,
he leaps out of the penalty box and punches someone
who has held a rubber chicken in front of his face. "It
wasn't the chicken. He spit at me," Sanderson explains.
In New York's Madison Square Garden he skates jaun-
tily to the penalty box after beating up a local hero.
Above him the overhangs are plastered with signs—most
of them are about Derek: "Derek is a Hairy Fairy;"
"Derek is Drek;" "You're Next Derek." It is a crescendo
of boos as Sanderson is almost in the box. But first, so
leisurely, he holds up both hands. Is he giving the fans
the finger? No, not at all. Incredibly, the first two

fingers on each hand are forming a V. Derek is giving the fans the peace sign.

They hate him—passionately, with no reservations. They don't think it's cute. Coyness is not for hockey fans. In Boston, they don't know what to make of him. The fans in the box seats wear T shirts. They have left no beer by the end of the game. They all would look comfortable in hard hats—even the bouffant ladies. They sneer at the opposition. Under other circumstances, perhaps at a busing demonstration, they would rip Sanderson apart because of his long hair and his peace signs. But at Boston Garden he is one of them and they accept him. Not quite with the love they've reserved for Bobby Orr, or the respect they give Phil Esposito. What the hell, he's a mixed-up kid. Every family has one like this. Accept him.

The third-line center. That's what he was for the Boston Bruins. He squired the cannon-fodder line, the one that does the dirty work against the opposition's best. Slow up the enemy, jab them a little, keep them busy. Soften them for Orr and Esposito. Is the St. Louis Blues' Garry Unger playing too well? Send out Sanderson to pick a fight with him, get them both chased off for fighting. You're well rid of Unger. Sanderson? Well, there's still Orr and Esposito.

There's always an Orr or an Esposito above him, above the hundreds of professional hockey players. How to get there, to get your name mentioned in the same breath, to swing with the big boys? If you're Derek Sanderson, you adopt a plan—a five-year plan—when you get to the big leagues. You know that your talent—and it is considerable—will be overshadowed by those who score more goals, or those who are faster, or those who are better loved.

The first inkling Derek Sanderson had that the good, the kind, and the just don't get their due came one day in Canada. His team, the Niagara Falls Flyers, was going to play an exhibition game against a Russian squad. His father, Harold, gave him some advice. "Run somebody," said Harold.

Harold Sanderson always gave advice to Derek Sanderson. Most of it was centered around this thought: Wind up better than I did, son. Harold is a small man, with darting eyes and sharp features.

"Hockey's a rough game in this country," he would tell little Derek. "If it's not worth fighting for, it's not worth winning."

"Sure I told him that," relates Harold. "Fighting builds a reputation. I told him to let them know you'll fight. I used to tell him, 'Derek, you don't take shit from anybody.'"

Yet, Harold Sanderson, as Derek remembers, "was a sensitive man. He could cry easily. He got emotional about things."

Derek laughs as he recalls some of his father's patriotic fervor of World War II. "Dad was off to fight 'the wily Hun,'" says Derek. "He was proud that he was in World War II before the Americans discovered it."

The war was a memory when Harold returned to Niagara Falls with a wife. He started as a floor sweeper and then Karen came along followed by Derek. The money was nothing in the Sanderson household. Caroline Sanderson would take the $40 a week Harold gave her. She knew he'd kept a little for beer money, but what the hell. The kids were clothed and fed and Harold worked hard.

But always it wasn't quite enough. Harold read: *Thirty Days to a More Powerful Vocabulary;* histories, biographies, newspapers. He argued over the working class and became a strong union man. He was at once a radical and a reactionary. The working class was being stepped on. Canada was being exploited by the United States. Get big business to open its pockets. But at the same time he believed the finest sort of person in the world was a WASP. The word didn't exist then, but the concept did. Canada for Canadians, said Harold. The work ethic, the Judeo-Christian heritage. These were the ideas really important, worth fighting for.

Harold remembers that he was one of seven children, and his "old man" always had a rink for them, a patch of ice to play on. "It's a matter of pride to be able to skate well in this country. It makes men out of boys," Harold explains.

Now the war was over and Harold was a man. They bought a house. "It wasn't in the best section of town, but it was ours," he says. He calls it a "wartime house," built quickly and cheaply. It had two stories. There were three bedrooms upstairs. And there was a backyard and a driveway. The backyard went back 110 feet and it was 50 feet long. A lot less than a regulation ice rink.

"There was only one indoor rink in this town," says Harold. "If you didn't have a backyard, you were beat." Presumably, being beat means no chance to get ice time, to skate and get experience for the ultimate—the chance of making it big in hockey.

There was a backyard, though. Harold still wasn't satisfied. He wanted the yard as big as possible, to simulate the dimensions of a real rink, the kind of rink he knew his son would have to make it on. So Harold went to his neighbors. How about joining backyards, he asked them. No fences. Just one long smooth stretch. In the winter it could be flooded. When it froze, there would be an area 200 feet long—just like the big leagues. However, the next door neighbors wanted their privacy and that was out.

Across the street lived a man from a construction company. The man had bulldozers. Harold spoke to him and asked how much it would cost to clear out the backyard, make it smooth and level. The man said he'd do Harold a favor. He'd send over the bulldozer on a slow day and clear out the area for nothing. And that's what he did. One day there was suddenly room for a mini-rink in the Sanderson's backyard.

When the weather grew cold, Harold would uncoil the hose that had been put away during the summer. He would spread a thin layer of water over the backyard, the beginning of a frozen surface. But often the hose was stiff. Harold would get a blowtorch, sometimes working two, three hours thawing out the hose and then spraying the yard. It takes an awful long time to water a yard so that it freezes.

"Sometimes I'd spray all night after coming home from work," says Harold.

While he sprayed, Caroline Sanderson would sit in the kitchen, smoking a cigarette and sipping her tea.

"I get my big heart, my worrying, and my nervousness from my mother," says Derek. "I also get my stubbornness from her."

There was, of course, a stove in the kitchen, and Derek claims there was something about that stove he'll never forget. It was the burners. "Don't touch them," Caroline would tell young Derek. "It's very hot. It'll burn you."

But Derek was fascinated with boiling water. He would stare at it, not comprehending what made the bubbles and the hissing. Whenever Caroline Sanderson noticed Derek staring at a pot boiling over the burner, she'd slap him.

"One day she was boiling milk," he says. "And it boiled over the top. I stared at it as it bubbled over and my mind went blank. I put my hand on the lid and clutched it. I just didn't want to let go. I held on to the lid a good four seconds. It was so hot it numbed me and I could see my skin smoking. The skin came off. My mother grabbed me and smacked me."

That was proof of love to the boy. It was a loving household, he remembers. There was closeness. Still, Derek wanted proof. One day he asked his father, "If a gunman came through the door and he said I'm going to kill either your son, your daughter, or your wife, what would you say?"

His father answered: "If I couldn't die first to save the three of you, I'd let him kill you children."

Derek's mother just smiled. Derek was shocked. "How? Why?" he asked.

"Look at it this way," explained Harold. "When Karen's twenty, she's going to get married and leave me. Then you'll get married and leave me, and old Harold will be right out the door. You're not going to put me in any old folks' home. Your mother—well, I'm all she's got. Your mother and I can always have more kids if something happened to you. But I can't have another Caroline. As much as I love the both of you, I'd take your mother. I wouldn't think twice about it. Your mother wouldn't say goodnight to me and walk out the door. I've got to stick with her."

Derek was fourteen years old when the conversation took place. By then, his life had been highly stylized. He put in fifteen hours a week toward hockey, either skating in the back, firing pucks over the frozen driveway, or playing kids' hockey. Harold had given him well-defined plans. You shoot the puck a hundred times, you rush back and forth fifty times, you spend an hour studying. As far as the hockey went, there was room for improvement. Harold, though, believed "I had to praise him before I criticized him." So first would come the pats on the back, then the critiques.

The work paid off. Derek developed a reputation as a good stickhandler, a clever player, a heady man on face-offs and killing penalties. There were even a few NHL clubs who expressed interest in the boy. He was now fifteen years old, time to start some heavy thinking about his future. That's right, about his future. When you're a hockey player in Canada, you've got to make the decision while you're a kid. Either it's up the ladder in the junior ranks or forget about the big time. This is a system that most Americans can't comprehend.

Say you're a basketball, football, or baseball player in the States and you're fifteen years old. Why, you'll simply continue with high school. There's no alternative. The high schools are the training grounds for the colleges, and the colleges are the training grounds for the pro leagues in these sports. But in Canada it's not the school teams that prepare a hockey player for the pros. It s in the junior system, where they can play more than sixty games a year, take midnight bus rides that go on for five hours after a game, and then show up for school the next morning. It's not the best system, but it's been the only one that works, the only one that prepares Canadian hockey players. There have been some concessions made to change the system.

Thinking members of Canadian Parliament were outraged that the juniors, in effect, were simply training grounds for the pros. While Derek was growing up in the late 1950s and early 1960s, about 80 percent of the players in the National Hockey League hadn't graduated from high school. They had been allowed to turn professional when they were eighteen, and for a boy from a scrubby dirt farm in Saskatchewan, or from the mines up in Sudbury, Ontario, the pros were one way out. A high school diploma wasn't going to do him much good down in the mines or on the farm anyway, and if you could make a living playing hockey, well, why not? It didn't seem to matter much that when their careers were over—and even if they made it to the NHL, their average playing time was only seven years—they weren't fit to earn any kind of living outside hockey. It didn't seem to matter, either, that at least one highly regarded youngster, who stayed in school until he was fifteen, couldn't even read or write. This particular player, Eddie Shack, couldn't sign his name. When asked for autographs, he'd produce a pad and a rubber stamp. It took time, but now Canadians can't turn pro until they're twenty years old. Of course, it also took a little pressure from the government, which threatened deep investigations into the Canadian junior system and its tie-in with the National Hockey League.

Derek's future was made easier for him when the Bruins moved a Junior B team into his neighborhood. He had finished midget play, and now was ready to take the next step, the leap into junior hockey. If there hadn't been a junior club in his area, he simply would have left home and gone to play where there was a team. Actually, Sanderson (and virtually every other young man in Ontario) hoped to make it to the Marlboros, a junior club affiliated with the Toronto Maple Leafs. Maple Leaf Gardens was the summit for all the good little boys in the province, just as Yankee Stadium was

Mecca for someone from the Bronx. The Marlies also had good money to pay, says Derek's father, "because they were owned by the Leafs." Because they had money, they could pay for the better players to come into Toronto. These kids they were paying $60 or $70 a week were supposed to be amateurs. And they were amateurs simply because they were called amateurs.

Does it seem strange that a fifteen-year-old would leave home just to play hockey? It doesn't to a Canadian household that wants its young hero to make it in hockey. It meant going to school in a strange city, often hundreds of miles from home, and it meant living either in a boardinghouse or with some family that wanted to pick up a few extra dollars a week (provided by the junior team), and it also meant going to a new school and making new friends.

But mostly it meant playing hockey, almost seventy games a year, when school was in session. And how many boys are going to stay in school under these conditions? Not many, and not many did. The vast majority, with money burning a hole in their blue jeans and usually a nifty old convertible and some teeny-boppers around, elected to quit school. Who was going to make intelligent decisions for them when they were far from home, or was going to give them sound advice? Yes, there were some coaches for junior clubs who really cared about their boys' future. And, perhaps, there were some gray-haired ladies who took in young hockey players as boarders who also could give advice to a teen-ager. But for the most part, when they left home they were on their own. The school adviser? He was part of a system that made sure the boy had enough free time to play hockey. Usually, the local junior team and its management was the most important product in the town. School officials looked the other way when classes were cut or a boy was late.

Derek, however, didn't fall into this trap. He found a junior team close to home. When Derek dropped out of high school, it was simply because he thought he was smarter than anyone else in it. Also, his grades were poor.

The junior team that wound up in Niagara Falls was led by Hap Emms, who also happened to be the general manager of the Boston Bruins. Every year the team was to have a free selection of one or two boys from the Niagara Falls area. Emms, though, didn't like Sanderson when the boy showed up at training camp to try out for the club.

Sanderson was selected, over Emm's objections. The man who chose him was the patriarch of the NHL, Weston W. Adams, Sr., president of the Bruins. Adams's father had a distinction: He owned the first United States team in the NHL. Over the years the Bruins became a dynasty, and there always was an Adams at the helm. Strange that Adams should take an interest in Derek. In temperament, language, background, and life-style they were opposites. One imagined Adams at home in a smoking jacket in an oak-paneled library. He was. But he also was a bit different from the other five powers that ran the NHL those days. As a young man he made heads turn when he took off in a stunt plane. At one time he claimed the New England altitude record in a biplane—reaching a height of 19,000 feet. Once, at an air show, his plane disintegrated in midair. His parachute opened when he was 100 feet above the ground. Adams didn't want to disappoint the 15,000

people. When he landed he climbed out of the parachute and quickly climbed into the cockpit of another
craft and continued the show.

That was all behind him, however, when he first
saw Derek Sanderson. The boy had a certain flair and
perhaps it took him back to the pre-oak-paneled days,
when he used to soar alone. He couldn't do that any-
more, of course. He had to maintain a certain dignity
as he carried on the Adams name. But Sanderson could
do it for him on the ice. The boy was fearless. So Adams
told Emms to take him.

During a practice in the camp, Harold and Caroline
Kennedy Sanderson were wandering under the stands.
They came across Emms and Adams. Emms performed
the obligatory introductions. It was the first time the
Sandersons had met the old man.

Adams smiled and said, "I want you both to know
that it wasn't him [nodding toward Emms] that chose
your boy, and it wasn't the scouts. It was me." Then
Adams added, "He's got the look of eagles, that boy. The
look of eagles."

Thus a relationship began between Derek, whom
the old man would call "Sandy," and Weston W. Adams,
Sr. In years to come, the two would become fond of each
other. The old man acted and felt paternal toward
Sandy. And one day they would break up.

But that was more than ten years away. Sanderson
had made it to the juniors and he was on his way, a
skinny kid who had developed a reputation as a brawler,
swearer, and wise guy. The kid, though, came to play.
Soon, he made the leap to the A team. His scoring and
assists increased, and his reputation spread. Derek was
bored with school.

"There are three things in every guy's life," Harold

Sanderson told him when Derek was sixteen. "There's social life, hockey, and school. You have to pick two of them. You can't do all three."

Derek picked the first two. He dropped out of school, and his father to this day believes it was justified. After all, you can only do two out of three.

His club was good enough to get to the Memorial Cup finals. The Memorial Cup is the Stanley Cup, the Super Bowl, the World Series, all wrapped up into one, for the junior championship of Canada. Every top scout goes to the Memorial Cup games. Most of the general managers from the NHL are there, too, and newspapers send their top reporters, and the radio and television networks give it broad coverage across Canada. Perhaps the Rose Bowl in the United States is closest to it. Close, but not more significant.

"We were going to play Edmonton," says Derek. "I'd been in some scrapes before, even been suspended— once for swearing, once for not obeying orders. And all I did against Edmonton was punch a guy in the mouth. I couldn't believe what happened—TV, radio, newspapers. For days. And it amazed me that one punch created all that hassle. And I said to myself that if you do sensational things, just once in a while, you become a household word."

That brings us back to the bit of advice Harold Sanderson offered young Derek before the exhibition game against the Russians.

"Do me one favor," said Harold. "Run somebody."

Derek did. The Russians were all older than the juniors they were playing against. In those days under international rules you were penalized if you threw a check at a player in his own end. The Russians never worried about this. They knew they were older and bigger than Sanderson's team, and anyway, they had the rules on their side.

"This one guy put his head down as he took the puck behind his net," relates Derek. "He's doing his number and I line him up when I'm at the blue line, sixty feet away. I take a run at him, really gathering steam, and I knock him out cold. Later, some newsmen asked me about it and I said I was sorry, that I'd forgotten about that international rule. But then I thought, the hell with it. 'I did it because my father told me to.' "

In Derek's words: "Bam, headlines. Sanderson creates international incident." More reinforcement and Derek filed it away.

A few days later there was a game against the Czechs. As sometimes happens when Derek is on the ice, there was a fight. "I had a guy in the corner and I was punching him and he started to spit at me. Now, I never had anyone spit at me before. But I knew that Europeans do that, that it shows complete contempt for you. So I punched him again. He started to run around. To them, it's not the manly thing to do, this fighting business. Their standards are different. Later in the game he speared me and started to spit again. So I reamed him with my stick. What an act, he started rolling on the ice, moaning and groaning. Next day, headlines again, international incident, that sort of thing."

And that's when it hit Derek Sanderson: "You don't have to be good. You've got to be notorious." All you've got to do is something outrageous, "just once in a while." At that moment, he could see his career take shape, a career that would see him on top one day because of those "once in a while" things that he would do by design.

"See, I always wanted to be liked," says Derek. "But you get more notoriety out of being knocked and hated.

It's a shame, but people live off that kind of stuff. I'm some sort of symbol to them, and they see me as evil. I realized it didn't matter then what people thought of me—good or bad. If some of them actually came to meet me, then they'd form a judgment based on the meeting, no matter how they prejudged me. They'd know me for myself. So what's the difference, really, what strangers think of you—except that in my case it paid. I figured the villain is as good, if not better than, the nice guy. I also learned that being the villain gave me complete freedom. No one was going to run after me to go to hospitals like they do with Bobby Orr. If I give people the finger or the arm in a game, they expect it. Hell— they need it."

TWO

THE FIVE-YEAR PLAN took shape in the summer of 1967, after Derek finished with junior hockey by leading the Ontario Hockey Association in scoring. He knew he was going to join a Boston Bruins team that had Bobby Orr aboard. Orr had won the rookie-of-the-year award and was already touted as the player of the future. And Esposito had recently been traded to Boston following a consistent 20-goal career with the Chicago Black Hawks. The Bruins were in their ascendancy, Sanderson knew, and he was only a rookie. He was twenty-one years old, had led the juniors in penalty minutes once and had led them in scoring once. That's an unusual combination.

"Maybe there were great players on the same team with Ruth and Gehrig," says Derek. "The point is, you never heard of them. They never got the ink. I knew it would be that way at Boston, with Orr and Esposito. I had to think of ways to get known."

Quite simply, Derek became outrageous. Reporters

flocked to him after a workout and he'd say something absurd. "I hustled the shit out of them," he explains, "and then I created this Frankenstein monster which I still can't shake."

The hustle started early. Derek came to camp with three jackets. The Nehru style was in, and he looked splendid wearing a Nehru jacket with a colorful turtle-neck. The next day he'd change jackets and sweaters. The third day he'd do the same. But by the fourth day he began mixing and matching—wearing the first day's jacket with the second day's sweater. He was twenty-one years old, lean and fit, and looked well in clothes. The Nehru jackets didn't cost him much. He had made a deal with a clothing store and got them cut-rate. He also had two pairs of shoes, "one black, one brown," and he matched them with his suits.

Soon, it appeared he had gone through fourteen different clothing outfits in a week. He was getting known as a clotheshorse. One day a reporter asked him, "Derek, are you blowing all your money on clothes?" Derek replied that indeed he was.

"Well, how many suits do you have anyway?" the reporter asked.

Derek answered: "I've got forty-one."

"You've got to be kidding. Forty-one?"

"Well, I told him that included the jackets," says Derek, "so I couldn't blame him for believing me. I mean, he couldn't go to my place and start counting all my suits. I didn't know how important this guy was, and that what he was going to write about me would have an important effect on my life. But I figured that if he was a Boston writer it would be important."

Then the writer asked how many pairs of slacks and Sanderson told him that sixty-five pairs of pants were hanging in the closet. How about shoes? Derek replied, "forty-five."

"I became a fashion plate overnight. I owe it all to Tom Fitzgerald, the guy who wrote the story. After that they started to write about my clothes and then they started to write about other things. I made the team and the season began and I had a reputation before I'd even done anything. So if I gave a fan the finger that was written about. If I got in a fight it suddenly became a bigger deal because it was me that was fighting and not some guy without forty-one suits. I was really getting known. The fashion page of some paper was doing a big spread on the latest in men's clothing. They asked me for my opinion on men's handbags, things like that. Now what the hell did I know about that sort of stuff. Here I am with three cut-rate Nehru jackets and I'm the big authority on fashion. I'm making eight grand a year. That's all, and that's a story, too. The guy who signed me was Emms, my old buddy from Niagara Falls. Emms was about to be fired as general manager of the Bruins and he told me, real confidential, that he was going to take care of me. The way he'd do that was to sign me to a three-year deal. No matter what happened, if my career ended because of an injury, I'd be taken care of for three years. So I signed, and got $8,000 for the first year, then $11,000 for the second, and $13,000 for the third. Essentially, that first year I played for about a hundred bucks a game. But I was suddenly a big deal. I could hardly keep up with my image. I got invited to some bachelor-of-the-year dinner and me, big swinger, had to go and buy a tux.

"Meanwhile, I was living in a boardinghouse in Saugus, and that's not too cool—not for a playboy on his way up. Saugus doesn't exactly sound very hip. Anyway one day I was driving and got caught in a traffic jam and this huge apartment building sign caught my eye. It read 'If you lived here you'd be home by now.' That blew my mind. I stopped, walked right in, and took a pad. It was 6 Whittier Place, Charles River Park."

To go with the fancy new address, Sanderson turned in some fancy skating. The Bruins were feeling better about things. Orr was definitely the finest defenseman in the game. Esposito had blossomed in his new surroundings. The club's hopes were bright. Sanderson had started the season as a regular, centering the third line with the first of the many right and left wings that would join him over the years. In his seventh game he appeared at the old Madison Square Garden, and got two goals. "You ought to start thinking about rookie-of-the-year," Esposito advised him. It was good advice, and it came from someone who had been screwed out of winning the award. When Esposito was a rookie for the Black Hawks in the 1963–64 season, he appeared in twenty-seven games. Or, rather, showed up for twenty-seven games. In many of those games he simply went out for one shift. He didn't play full time in more than half. Yet, league rules stipulate that in order to be considered a rookie, a player may not have participated in more than twenty-five games. Esposito didn't know this, and his coach, Billy Reay, never bothered telling him. Each time Reay sent him over the boards during a losing cause was another game that counted in Esposito's totals. In Esposito's first full season, the 1964–65 campaign, he got twenty-three goals and would have been a prime candidate for rookie honors. But he was ineligible.

Sanderson didn't have to worry. He played in seventy-one games and got twenty-four goals, adding twenty-five assists for forty-nine points. He was named the NHL's top rookie.

In his second year the transformation was continuing. There was a white llama rug in the apartment, which he now describes as decorated in "nouveau riche." He had a mustache; he wore white boots. People asked him whether he was emulating Joe Namath. "Who's he?" Sanderson replied.

Derek needed some wheels to go along with this. He realized that every three years Cadillac altered its basic styling. But for those three years, one Caddy looked much the same as another. So he bought a three-year-old Cadillac for $4,000. When people would ask him about it, he'd tell them it was brand new. Even at $4,000, it cost him practically his whole take-home pay. Two years later, he sold it for the same $4,000.

The heavy tipping followed. "If I was in a cab and the guy recognized me, I'd give him a four- or five-dollar tip," relates Derek. "That was the price I had to pay. If he didn't know me from a hole in the wall, well, okay, but that'll cost him. If a guy served me really well in a bar or a restaurant, he might get a twenty-five dollar tip. I've given as much as a $100 tip to a bartender.

"You see, my policy always was: tip the little people—the doormen, the waitresses, the cabbies, the bartenders. They're around all the time, not the bosses. These are the people who talk about you and can help you."

Sanderson's hair and flair were also making hockey fans talk about him. With the possible exception of the Hawks' Bobby Hull, he quickly became the most-approached player by newsmen after a game. If it was an honest evaluation of an opponent the press wanted, or if it was an appraisal of a teammate or even a coach, Sanderson was available. It didn't matter that some of the things he said to one reporter would contradict what he said to another. Paper appeared out of notebooks, pencils were clutched between fingers, and note-taking was on. Derek would call another coach "bush" or label an opponent as "no-talent." He violated hockey's code that you never knock anyone. It was refreshing, especially for a press that had been accustomed to dealing with close-mouthed players, virtually all of whom were Canadian and brought up in an atmosphere that kept all the old hokey, hockey traditions. When you won, you didn't brag. When you lost, you didn't knock. None of this meant anything to Sanderson. He would talk about a goalie's weak points; he would label another player a chicken.

He'd say things to the press that would make Esposito, who sat alongside Sanderson, wince and sometimes hide. Sometimes Esposito would simply look at Sanderson, shake his head, and mumble, "Derek, Derek, oh, Jesus." There would be games when Sanderson had been a zero factor. But where were the reporters and tape recorders? Near Sanderson, who'd sit there with his knees spread apart, wearing a soaked pair of long johns, dragging on a cigarette (which he invariably grubbed from someone who had his favorite brand), and holding court. Orr would be in hiding, usually in the out-of-bounds trainer's room, making believe he was taking a whirlpool treatment. Esposito was agreeable and chatty and would also have some newsmen hovering about. But Sanderson indisputably held center stage.

"Geez, I thought Emile Francis had more class than that," he'd say after a fight with the Rangers' Ed Giacomin, when Giacomin suggested Coach Francis had placed a bounty on Sanderson's head.

"That Cournoyer's gutless," he would say about the Canadiens' Yvan Cournoyer after the player was beaten up by one of the Bruins' bruisers and was no factor in the game.

"The fans are animals," he said after being booed.

On the ice he'd get into a fight. Lots of players get
into fights. But when Sanderson was involved, it usually
was a beauty. There'd be none of this pushing and shov-
ing. The opponent would stare at Sanderson for a long
second, wondering whether a punch should be thrown,
wondering if Sanderson would start something. And
suddenly Sanderson would be all over him. No fancy-
dan baloney with jabs, no feinting, no gratuitous shoves.
Sanderson leaped and flailed, punches coming from
everywhere and every time, it seemed, the opponent was
caught off guard. These punches were meant to hurt,
bare-knuckled shots that were incredibly on target in the
only unprotected area—the face. Did anyone see when
the gloves flew off? No. But the gloves had been shaken
off (the first sign that an opponent is willing to fight
after the stick is dropped) and punches were coming
faster and faster. There was a desperation about the
punching, a strange mindlessness in a player who had
raised cunning to an art form. "Don't take shit from
anybody," his father had told him. The player would be
down, and still Sanderson would sock him, not pulling
the punch, not consciously attempting to inflict pain,
simply intent on stopping the other guy from landing
even one punch.

Yet, there would be times when he would square
off, cock his right fist, and let it fall to his side. Then he'd
skate away and smirk as if to say, "you thought I was
going to do it, but I've got my reasons for not killing you
now." Other times he'd laugh when a player shoved him,
and he would turn his back with disdain. Sometimes,
he'd be caught in a penalty after tripping someone. On
his way to the penalty box, Derek would shove the other
player out of his way. Or he might even give the guy a
crack across the ankle with a stick.

For a man who dreaded this "Frankenstein monster" he was a long way from trying to kill it. At once he hated it—and nurtured it. He was unpredictable, yet he claimed he was in control. That was highly unlikely. It is likely that Sanderson himself didn't know how he was going to react in a given situation.

"The image started to take control, and it got out of proportion," says Derek. "So I sort of became a recluse, in my fashion. I raised my price for appearances from $100 to $1,000. This let me cut the requests from fifteen a week down to two. Then I asked $1,500 an appearance and I was getting asked only twice a month. People were after me for Kiwanis, church clubs, car salesmen, Boy Scouts. But I wasn't about to show up for the Boy Scouts. They've got enough people looking after them or trying to help them. I wanted things, groups, where people weren't looking after them. Things like tough kids, juvenile delinquents. They're not as fashionable as Boy Scouts or Kiwanis. I realized I had to do that sort of work on my own. So instead of saying no to all the offers and looking like a bad guy, I just made my price so high that nobody could afford it."

More than anything else, though—transcending the fighting, the wise cracks, the goals—was the well-founded belief that Derek Sanderson was the greatest swordsman in the world of sports. A swordsman is jock terminology for a guy who has all the women he wants. Derek had them, and he loved it. He had no reservations about flaunting them, either. If *Life* magazine showed up with a photographer, there was Derek posing on his round bed with his roommate, a stewardess named Judy Martin who, he claims, was "one of the three great loves in my life."

The rest he dismisses as "just fun." Sanderson, the

moralizer, insists, "I never made it with anyone who was married." Then he stops, thinks, and corrects himself. "Oh, yeah, just one—but she was separated." The name he drops of this woman would make a million men lapse into fantasy. Sanderson insists that when he has been with the women he loved, he was faithful. There are, however, an awful lot of temptations for an athlete, and he was never one to turn down a beautiful woman—or even two, simultaneously. And he didn't mind being seen with them or talking about women, who he gratuitously characterized as "broads, chicks, and women."

It may be, as he claims, that he didn't lose his virginity until he was twenty. But he quickly made up for lost time. This easy way with women—and the ease in getting them—has created in Sanderson and other athletes a very rigid value system of women.

"I wouldn't let a daughter of mine marry an athlete," he says. "They have a distinctly low opinion of women. In my case, the girls started coming around when I turned pro. They got caught up in the American syndrome of athlete worship. Generally, athletes use women as objects. There's a simple reason for this. Their egos are too big and they're too insecure. They've learned they can make it, and that's how women have shown themselves to athletes. It's the way they've wanted and expected to be treated. They've demanded to be treated like this. Most of the guys aren't sensitive enough or intelligent enough to get beneath the surface, inside, to see what she's like. And why should they? They don't realize a woman's a delicate animal and has to be treated with kid gloves."

The well-detailed sex life of athletes is no myth. Ask visiting basketball players in New York about the girl who stops them in the hotel lobby and wants to go to their rooms to say her "rosary." The funniest thing about this girl is that she's Jewish. Then there's the girl who works only hockey players and who once screamed at a New York Ranger, calling him a "fag son of a bitch" after he refused to let her into his apartment. And there's also Chicago Shirley, who will bestow her favors on anyone connected with sports—referees, stickboys, equipment managers, broadcasters. Indeed, she calls them up.

"By any standards our sex life is bizarre," Sanderson concedes. "And so the athlete takes the easy way out, the handy stuff, rather than get involved with a woman and caring for her, or concerned for her. He'll forget the one that's worth really trying for, and he'll screw the one that's easy."

"Why do I like Derek Sanderson?" asks an extraordinary woman who has just met him at the Playboy Club in Boston. She had been seen at some games, parading around during whistle stoppages (when all eyes would be on her), exhibiting one of the largest bosoms on the eastern seaboard. Now she is mulling over the question as she clutches Derek's hands. "I think it was his animalism," she says. "I heard he was some kind of animal."

She adds, "But what I liked mostly was that he played so hard to get. We never could get together. He always was so busy. This turned me on. Other guys were always running after me. I had to chase him." Then she turns to Derek and asks, "Are we going to Acapulco this weekend?"

She soon leaves for a modeling engagement and a bunny hops to his table.

"How about some breakfast later on?" he asks. It is 4 P.M. and bunnies get off about midnight. Breakfast is their term for a post-work snack.

"Gee, I don't know," she says. She is about twenty

years old and exquisitely beautiful. Perhaps she is a college girl. She does have a husband.

"Hey, I'll send my car over for you," he tells her. "This way no one has to know our business."

"Well, I guess it'll be all right. Okay," she says, finally.

"Good, so I'll pick you up at twelve and we'll go over to Daisy's for something. What time do you have to be in. Say two o'clock?"

"I suppose so," she answers.

"He gets a little nervous after two, huh?" asks Derek.

"I'd guess so," she answers. "I've never done anything like this before."

Derek has reached the stage where bunnies and models are common fare. The majority of the swinging athletes, though, get their kicks at their hotels.

"I don't know how they find out where our hotels are," he says. [It really is easy. Most teams' yearbooks give the names of hotels the teams visit when they're on the road.] Usually the girls call you on the phone first. Some just knock on the door. 'Hey, remember me, I met you at Bachelors III,' they'll say. Hell, maybe they saw me sitting there and figured I'd remember the place if not the face. Anyway, it doesn't matter what the excuse is. If they're good-looking, they come through the door. None of the groupies, though, is ever good-looking. A super good-looking woman just doesn't hang around hotels. She's like a well-tuned athlete. She can get it any time. She gets stared at enough, gets enough propositions, so that she doesn't need your aggravation, putting herself in a demeaning position for you."

The groupies—those ladies of an hour, who follow the athletes from town to town or simply camp in hotels and wait for the next batch of players to arrive—come in all ages. "From fifteen to forty," says Derek, "married, single."

"Hockey players," says Sanderson, "are straighter than most athletes. A lot of guys don't care how old the girls are. Hockey players, though, are straighter than baseball players, who are probably the freakiest of all. They take anything. Football players? They're the most brutal. They're animals. Their demands are ugly. They get the craziest women."

Then there was the lady in Oakland who simply had to meet Derek. She bribed the bellhop in an empty room and he returned the favor by letting her into Derek's room—he thought. Instead, he inadvertently opened the door to the room next to Derek. No one was in and she hid in a closet.

A few hours later one of the Bruins walked in and went to the closet to hang up his coat. He saw arms and legs and started to kick. He punched her in the head and kneed her. She started to scream, "I'm a girl, I'm here to sleep with you." Then she said, "Derek?"

"No," the player replied.

Then he told her to get lost, that he was a married man. She gathered herself together and said, "Okay, but can you find Derek for me?"

Privacy has never seemed particularly important to athletes once they've had a few drinks. At a bachelor party for a young Giant football player several years ago, the bridegroom was ushered into a smart East Side apartment where he found two naked beauties awaiting him on the floor.

Even hockey players, the most conservative of the sporting fraternity, have their public moments. There was the time in Sweden, during the famed series against the Russians, when a bunch of Team Canada superstars found themselves in a nightclub that featured live sex shows. A recruit from the audience was found, and one of North America's heroes exhibited himself in a way never seen on the game of the week.

"We're always being challenged to a round of sex," claims Derek. "They want to see if they can beat you." One woman who didn't succeed was one of New York's top madams, who made a small fortune writing her memoirs. She wound up in Canada, and one night took on several players. But there was one bachelor she gave two hours of her time, and she couldn't arouse him. She came out sweating, shook her head, and screamed, "The man's a goddam animal. I did everything he asked and nothing happened."

The so-called swinging scene began in earnest for Derek after he hooked up with Joe Namath in Bachelors III, a dark, cheerless bar. Namath already had a reputation as the sports world's most sincere swinger, who had boasted that the night before the Jets' Super Bowl upset over Baltimore he had gone to bed with "a bottle and a broad." Sanderson had been playing only two years when Namath was looking for a partner in Boston to open the New England branch of Bachelors III, a restaurant he owned in New York with two other people. The New York restaurant turned out to be frequented by those whom football czar Pete Rozelle labeled undesirables. Namath needed a key Boston name to launch the operation, and the names suggested to him were Bobby Orr, Tony Conigliaro, Ken (Hawk) Harrelson, and Sanderson. Orr was too quiet, Conigliaro too cocky, Harrelson too flakey. That left Derek. Derek agreed, so long as he could bring in some of his own people. He engaged Jimmy McDonough and Joe Cimino, both young law students, both with saloon experience, and wise beyond their years. McDonough's father was a kingmaker in Massachusetts politics. McDonough had also been a bartender while going to school. Cimino, who was to be the manager, was "honest as the day is long," according to Derek. He also "kept out all the weight—the drunks, the bums, the hookers. Everything was going to be on the up and up. I didn't want the kind of people coming in who went to Namath's place in New York."

Before long, Derek was making $30,000 a year out of Bachelors III. It was practically three times his salary for playing hockey. He made sure he was around. He didn't want to be an absentee landlord. With his face, now becoming well known, and his reputation, making him somewhat infamous, Sanderson was getting the notoriety he had demanded. Things came, he took them. One night a girl walked into Bachelors, pulled up her sweater, and asked him to sign his name around her nipple. The fun and games started to get serious.

"I'd be leaving a game. As soon as I got out the dressing room door, girls would be grabbing me. One fourteen-year-old kid, she grabbed my crotch, I swear. They were tearing off bits of my clothing, stuffing their phone numbers into my pockets." Before long, Derek had his car parked on the ramp that led into the dressing room area. In one leap he was into his car and away from the clutches of screaming mothers and daughters. He had found temporary shelter.

Still, they wouldn't leave him alone. "There were distinctly different types, but it all came down to the same thing. They wanted to see how good you were. There was the New York chick, fast, confident. She didn't give a damn who you were. She was cool. Then there was the pessimistic type. They couldn't stand me before they'd met me because of what they'd read or heard. Then there were some who we'd meet only because we're players, and they would go through all the motions except when it came to getting down to doing it they'd say no. It was almost as if they'd lead us on, and then say 'no' just to prove they were different. But they were really showing they were just like everyone else."

There were others who would go out and suddenly threaten to get a boy friend or a husband to fight. "But what they were doing out with you in the first place they don't explain," says Derek.

All this created in Sanderson a very special view of women. "If this hadn't happened, I probably would be married by now," he explains. "But after half a dozen years as a pro you might as well forget about getting married while you're playing. You couldn't meet a straight-on chick if your life depended on it. Most players are married before they make the big time. If not, then they get married after a lot of years of screwing around, after they've had their fill." Other famed swingers, notably Namath and the Rangers' Rod Gilbert, have also spoken of the impossibility of being married while still a superstar. It's different, perhaps, for players who became prominent but already were married. But once a handsome young bachelor is a hero, he doesn't suddenly want to give up all the perquisites of stardom. And the intelligent ones realize that just because you're married the offers and the looking don't stop. So they have decided to wait until their playing careers are over before going to a minister.

It is, of course, difficult to remain faithful even if you've been married and get to the big leagues. Many of the players are married by the time they're twenty or twenty-one years old. If they've come from small towns, they've married the local beauty, perhaps Miss Moose-jaw or Miss Elmira, and suddenly the athlete is thrust on center stage. He is now playing for one of the world's largest cities, and he is traveling easily across two countries, from coast to coast. His vista is broadened. His wife's remains the same. Thus, while he grows, meets important people (yes, the wealthy, too, love to get close to athletes, to invite them to the club for a round of golf), and goes to important places, Miss Elmira sits back home in the rented house and converses with other players' wives. Her circle is limited, her room for growth is circumscribed. She remains a housewife and mother, while the player is surrounded by a world he had only dreamed about.

Hang around a club long enough and you'll hear about this player being a "family man" or that one who just "likes to sit around the house." The point is, these are the exceptions. If they weren't, they wouldn't have the reputations for being nice guys.

Derek appreciates the pressure that hockey's women have. He concedes that "a lot of them are bothered that other women approach me right in front of them. Some of them have told me, 'I don't want to go out with you any more. It's too much of a hassle. You're always signing autographs. I'll go out with a bank clerk. It's much easier.' It's not the popularity they object to. They understand that you're known. It's the notoriety. It's the fact that when you're out with them you're not theirs. You belong to other people."

As it does for many male fans, hockey often brings out the worst in women. Perhaps it is because they can be faceless while at the same time telling off someone who's famous that makes athletes objects of scorn or affection.

There are the nasty ones, too, "who wait for you in
the lobby or at your car, or attempt to pick you up in a
bar. If you're married and you tell them to leave you
alone, they'll phone up a player's wife after being re-
jected and tell her to check her husband's room. They
tell the wife the player won't be in, that he's sleeping
around. Hell, I've seen some of these nuts slip a contra-
ceptive into a guy's jacket pocket just so his wife will
see it when he gets home. I've seen some of them slip a
pair of panties or a garter belt into a guy's suitcase while
it's standing in the lobby. And a lot of these guys get in
trouble, and they haven't done anything."

Players today are warned of possibly dangerous
alliances by the league's security chief, a perceptive former FBI agent named Frank Torpey. He has explained
to the married players the possibility of extortion—for
money, or perhaps a favor—if they get involved with the
wrong sort of woman. And of course the players are re-
minded of the baseball player, Eddie Waitkus, who got
shot in a hotel room by a disgruntled lady fan.

Sanderson has been in some scrapes, he admits.
"A guy pulled a knife on me in a bar because I once beat
up one of his favorite players. Another time someone
pulled a gun on me in Oakland because he didn't like
what he read about me in a newspaper column. The
story was about how tough I was. 'Shoot me, go ahead,'
I told him. He backed off."

What does all this do to a player's mind—to anyone's
mind? It all adds up. Slowly, things come together—the
pressures, the fans, the hard knocks, and the crazy
women. The first hint that it had affected Derek came
in his third season.

"Things were going super," he explains. "I was finally getting some recognition as a player, not for just

being a flake. And I met Judy. I'd never been in love before, really. I could see my future taking shape, getting the money I wanted. My contract was up and I knew I'd be in line for a healthy raise under a new deal. I was starting to get all the things I'd planned for. I was flying to a game somewhere and suddenly it hit me: I was scared to death. I thought that all this could suddenly end, just when I had what I always dreamed about—the love, the money, the success, the fame. I didn't want it to end. Who knows, maybe I felt guilty about taking, always taking. The success I had, maybe I believed it wasn't deserved. But I became scared shitless about flying."

Judy thought this was amusing. She was, after all, a stewardess for American Airlines. That didn't last long, though, not after airline officials saw her compromising pose in Derek's bed in the *Life* color spread.

"The flying—that's what started me drinking. I'd take ten, twelve shots straight. Anything, V.O., Canadian Club, Seagram's 7. After a while I got it down to a science so I'd know how much to drink so that when I'd get on the plane I'd pass out. I knew that if it was a short flight I'd sleep less if I took fewer drinks. Once I realized I could do it on a regular basis I was more relaxed. I learned to live with it. I had tried Librium and Valium and they didn't work. If I were on the ground and took them they would have knocked me out. But I was so hyper they didn't help me on the airplanes. Only the drinking did."

Derek flew, and he did begin to receive recognition for his talents. He became hockey's most famous—and most dangerous—penalty-killer. He did well in the playoffs, once leading everyone in goals and another time in penalties. He spoke often about his new image, and how he was attempting to shake the hedonistic image he had acquired. A magazine went so far as to title an article on him, "The Beatification of Derek Sanderson." He was not quite so outrageous as he used to be.

The treadmill refused to stop, though. And one day he went through an emotional upheaval.

"I started coughing up the blood in March, 1972," he says. "It came out of everywhere. I guess it was a combination of things. I was having problems with my love affair. It was on the rocks. One day Judy wanted to be a housewife, then she wanted to be an actress. We couldn't get together. The blood, the doctors said, was from colitis, caused by nerves. It settled in my stomach. It made me weak and lightheaded, no stamina."

Suddenly, being an athlete at center stage held terror for him. The fun and games were over. "I was manic-depressive. I didn't talk to the trainers, to my parents, to friends, to my attorney, to players. I thought they were all trying to screw me. A fan would come up to me and I'd curse him. They must have hated me, not realizing what I was going through. But I hated people staring at me. I thought everyone was against me. If I went into a restaurant, I thought someone was trying to poison my soup. I thought it was all over, that I was going to take a half gainer off the Mystic River Bridge."

Everything became a threat to Derek. He recalls, with the terror still showing in his eyes, "a woman coming at me with a pair of scissors to cut off some of my hair. I thought she was going to stab me. I was scared."

So near the end of the season, Derek entered a $200-a-day suite at Massachusetts General Hospital. It was as much for his nerves as his colitis. The doctors told him his play was finished for the time being. But, according to Derek, "the team suggested that I be al-

lowed to live in the hospital, and would it be okay if I
left for practices and the games, as long as I followed a
regimented diet. So I had this room with a fireplace and
a view of the River Charles. No visitors, seclusion. I'd
play, then I'd go back to the hospital."

Derek did not miss a game that season ("It was
a season without injury, so I played seventy-eight
games"). He credits the team's assistant trainer, John
Forristall, and a teammate, Mike Walton, with helping
him through.

"Forristall had been through a depression before,"
explains Derek. As for Walton, he is perhaps the only
athlete who got traded because he had a psychiatrist
verify he was unhappy in the city he was playing. That
happened in Toronto, where Walton was considered one
of the stars of the future. He had even married the boss's
niece. But he was depressed there. He underwent treatment, then appealed to the president of the league, Clarence Campbell, to get him traded. Campbell interceded
after the Leafs refused to deal him, and Walton wound
up in Boston. He earned the nickname "Shakey" from
his new teammates.

Walton told Derek: "Listen to me. I'm the only one
on this club who's got papers to prove he's sane." So
Walton and Sanderson would spend hours talking about
Derek's depression, which had the same symptoms as
Walton's. Eddie Johnston, the number two goalie, mean-
while found a nickname for Derek. It was "Twilight."

One of the keys to his recovery, he says, is the fact
that the doctor was "nonchalant" about it. "The first
time we met we joked around. The second time, we
got serious." The way Derek remembers it, the doctor
finally said to him, "You're okay. You're not sick, just
goofy. You're your own worst enemy." And that was that,

according to Derek. No long analysis, not even another visit.

Derek was finally healthy again and the fact that, two months later, he was on another Stanley Cup champion team helped. He needed his sanity for what was going to happen next.

Three

THE WORLD HOCKEY ASSOCIATION, unlike Derek Sanderson, started with a whimper. No bang accompanied the exclusive disclosure in May, 1971, in a Hollywood, Fla., newspaper that a new hockey league was being formed. Indeed, almost a year would go by before Sanderson even cared about the league—or the league about Derek.

Fittingly, the man who put the WHA together and lured the players was born in Shanghai. His name is Dennis Murphy, a portly, jovial sports executive who when thirty was the youngest mayor in California (Buena Park) and who founded the American Basketball Association, the rival of the entrenched National Basketball Association.

"I realized after Harry Truman got elected that because everyone says you can't do something doesn't make it so," says Murphy.

Murphy started the WHA because he couldn't get a long-term contract out of the Floridians, the Miami

ABA team he served as general manager. But for several years he had been making inquiries about hockey franchises in North America. Hockey was the nation's booming spectator sport, undergoing greater percentage increases than baseball, football, or basketball. His knowledge of civic affairs made it easy for him to find out such important factors as population, weather, and the demographics of urban areas.

When he realized he would be leaving basketball, he went back to California and contacted an old friend, Gary Davidson, a handsome blond lawyer who was the ABA's first president. Murphy was the man who organized sports leagues; Davidson took care of the legal difficulties.

"I think we ought to start a new hockey league," Murphy told Davidson.

The pair talked for a day and Murphy then went back to Miami to conclude his business with the basketball team.

Late in the season, Murphy discovered that the American Hockey League was having a meeting in Freeport, Bahamas. There was talk of putting an AHL team in Florida. A friend of Murphy's, Bernie Rosen, who was sports director of Channel 4 in Miami, decided to cover the meeting. Dennis went along on the flight.

Murphy told the assembled hockey executives he was a reporter. "Really, they just assumed I was," he explains. "I told them I was with Bernie. I tagged along and asked questions."

AHL officials were glad to be cooperative. After all, if they were indeed going to move to Florida, why not be nice to some visiting TV dignitaries?

Among the guests was Emile Francis, the general manager-coach of the New York Rangers of the NHL whose club ran Providence of the AHL.

"He was one of the guys I asked a lot of questions," says Murphy. "He didn't know who the hell I was, but he was very obliging. I asked him about all the players in the minors, and their contracts, and how binding the contracts were."

Francis unwittingly responded, as did other NHL potentates. Murphy soon found out that "there were dozens of really good minor leaguers who never made it to the NHL because there just wasn't room for them."

This helped convince Murphy that there was enough talent to go around, but he had to find out how binding the contracts were. He returned to California and found an attorney named Steve Arnold, who had left New York where he had had a celebrated clash with Francis. Arnold and a partner, Marty Blackman, had infuriated Francis by representing four key Rangers—Brad Park, Walt Tkaczuk, Vic Hadfield, and Jean Ratelle—and doubling their salaries. At one point in the negotiations Francis had become so incensed that he took back Park's skates.

Murphy asked Arnold if a new league could go and Arnold responded positively. Then he wondered if it could get NHL players and Arnold answered "yes." But could the contracts be broken? Arnold replied that in his view, there was no way those contracts could stand up in court.

"We weren't talking about long-term contracts, the definitive ones that a player signed agreeing to play for x-number of years," says Murphy. "We were talking about the one-year deals. But every contract had the option clause and that's what I was concerned about."

Murphy discovered that most players had only one-year or two-year deals. In other words, they could be ready to jump by the fall of 1972. Arnold estimated that between fifty and sixty players would be willing to jump leagues.

Davidson and Murphy talked some more and agreed that they'd be willing to spend as much as $100,000 between them to try to get the league organized. Murphy returned to Florida and discovered that, prematurely, the story of his intentions had broken. He had no choice but to announce that, in fact, there was a WHA.

"I heard that Francis saw me on television and recognized me, and that he said, 'the son a bitch.' "

For the next three months Murphy went up and down the eastern seaboard of North America, visiting forty cities, talking to more than 100 groups. He started with the premise that a new league needed the three major markets—New York, Chicago, and Los Angeles. That was required before you could even begin talking to a TV network for the sale of a package. Murphy knew the ABA had been badly hurt because it didn't have teams in Chicago or Los Angeles, and that the league's attractiveness for a TV sponsor had diminished.

On the other hand, he knew that the three cities already had NHL teams, and that "as much as possible, we wanted to stay away from the NHL cities." So he looked at Cleveland, Cincinnati, Baltimore, Atlanta, and Quebec. The last city he knew would be no problem. The city of Quebec had for years chafed under the handicap of being No. 2 in the province to Montreal. It wanted a major league team of its own.

In New York Murphy spoke to many different people, including Max Zaslofsky, the old basketball player, and Roy Boe, who owned the Nets of the ABA. Boe finally put in with the NHL—and ironically was to lose eight players to the WHA.

After his trek in the East, Murphy went back to California and started doing the West. Most people turned him down. They were worried that it would be too hard and costly a battle against the fabulously successful NHL.

"But I knew that the progress hockey was making was unreal," says Murphy. "Most major cities had secondary arenas, but with new ones being planned. Hockey was lucrative as hell. The owners were making *beaucoup* money. Heck, the cost of a franchise went from $2 million to $6 million in three years."

One of the keys to the new league's development was the need for a solid hockey man, someone well acquainted with the prickly thorns of the hedge surrounding the NHL. In short, the league needed a man who could do battle on the NHL's level. A "breakthrough," in Murphy's words, occurred when he was put in touch with Bill Hunter of Edmonton, known variously as "Wild Bill" and "Mr. Hockey of Western Canada." That last, restrictive definition didn't diminish Murphy's enthusiasm for Hunter.

"We hit it off immediately, especially since Hunter said he'd pay his own way to come to Los Angeles to meet me," Murphy explains.

Hunter had had his fights with the NHL, mostly over junior hockey and the NHL's control of the juniors. He had many allies in Canada, including Ben Hatskin of Winnipeg, who was known as "the corrugated-box king of Manitoba."

With Hunter's wild-eyed enthusiasm, and Hatskin's supreme confidence (he was the man, after all, who drafted Bobby Hull) the league began to take concrete shape with important alliances in Canada.

Hatskin was a no-nonsense bear of a man. At first he didn't want to be bothered. When Murphy invited him to Los Angeles, Hatskin claimed he had to go out and buy some new clothing, and didn't want to go shopping. He eventually was convinced by his friend Hunter. The pair made an intriguing team. Hatskin is a man who says, "I'm mean. I growl and yell. When I have to talk my way through a business deal, I can talk. If I have to push my way through a deal, I push."

An organizational meeting was planned for Los Angeles, and Murphy and Davidson could finally talk about getting some money back. There would be a $5,000 cost to have an option on a team in the WHA. Once a club took its option, it would also have to turn over $25,000 to the Murphy-Davidson duo. This, in effect, was a finder's fee and covered expenses the pair had undertaken.

Before the meeting, an executive Murphy knew from the ABA called and asked if he could attend. He said he was representing some people from Atlanta. "Sure," Murphy replied.

"The guy took notes throughout the meetings," Murphy recalls. "After he left I got word from several different sources that he was there as a spy for the NHL. I really couldn't believe it, so I called him in Atlanta, and asked him if it were true.

"Sure," the man told Murphy. "Everybody's got to make a living."

"He was a little apologetic about it," says Murphy. "But I didn't like the idea, especially since he was at the hotel at our expense."

There were spies in the WHA midst from this time

on, Murphy insists. He claims that private detectives shadowed him and Davidson and goes so far as to say his phone was tapped.

"I was hearing funny beeps on the phone," he relates. "And I had the thing fixed three times. The phone company called it 'interference,' but I'm sure the NHL was bugging it. It's just that so many things seemed to be happening: The spy at the meeting, the detectives, and my bank phoning me and telling me they've been getting calls about me."

There were to be other rumors later on, once the league established itself. The most persistent story concerned Charles O. Finley and his on-again, off-again coach, Fred Glover, and the WHA's Cleveland Crusaders. Glover was dismissed by Finley, the one-man ruler of the California Golden Seals of the NHL. Soon, ironically, Glover wound up with the Crusaders, who had raided two of Finley's players. Within a matter of days, Glover quit the Crusaders and jumped back to the Seals. Many people in the WHA claim that Glover's job was to infiltrate the Crusaders and determine how many more Golden Seals were thinking of jumping.

"Glover was at our draft meetings," says Murphy, "and the NHL knew all the moves we were thinking of making. I have to assume he was still working for Finley, but I don't know for sure."

Later on there would be even more suspicion of sabotage. Once the new league had established itself it announced it was going to play a series against the Czechs, the world champions. It would have followed the highly publicized Team Canada (NHL)-Soviet Union series and would have gone a long way toward giving the new league credibility—at home and abroad. But the United States and Canadian amateur hockey associations—which have to sanction international matches in their respective countries—turned down the series after all the groundwork had been done and agreements made.

Even before the league played a game, though, it was becoming somewhat paranoid about the NHL, perhaps with justification. One of the WHA's breakthrough meetings occurred in New York in late fall of 1971. It followed the first major meeting on the West Coast, and for the first time brought the league under the scrutiny of the major television, magazine, and newspaper markets of the United States. At the meeting the league spoke of its plans for a twelve-team league to start in October, 1972. The first puck was to be dropped at the new arena in Miami. It was to be an orange puck, a radical departure from the traditional black. There would be an NHL team in New York (the key city, as everyone knew) and for the first time major league hockey would come to the Deep South. Yet, no sooner had the announcement been made about the New York press conference for the WHA than the NHL said it was going to have a major meeting a few days later.

The WHA conference created a whole new image for the league. An extraordinary turnout of more than sixty newsmen was at the Americana Hotel and the new league in a sense was launched in the public mind.

Then came the NHL meeting. For years the older league had said it didn't plan to expand again before 1973 at the earliest, and probably wouldn't do so until 1974. Yet, it announced that it was going to expand in 1972—by coincidence in New York and the Deep South. Strangely, a franchise was awarded to New York (Long Island actually), but not to an individual. Thus, the move was seen as an attempt to steal the WHA's thunder. The NHL wanted a second team in the huge metropolitan area to take away the impact of the WHA's move there. As far as the South was concerned, another franchise was awarded to Atlanta.

Campbell was asked if this move to New York and Atlanta was indeed made to keep out the WHA. Thinking of the anti-trust repercussions of his answer, he replied, "If it has that effect, so be it." Then he was asked why the league moved up its timetable ahead of schedule. "Does Macy's tell Gimbel's?" he asked.

Still, the WHA pressed on. It demanded that its owners have plenty of money ("one of the mistakes we made in the ABA was not getting people rich enough to run teams," Murphy conceded). Then, of course, it started looking for players. The league knew that one of the keys in providing players was Alan Eagleson, the head of the NHL Players Association. Eagleson, a clever Toronto lawyer who represented Bobby Orr among many clients, welcomed the WHA. But he didn't deliver any players to it.

Eagleson claimed in every case where a deal fell through that "the up-front money" wasn't right or "the escrow in the banks" wasn't right.

"That didn't help us," says Murphy. "He should have got the Players Association behind it with money to help out. This was going to be the greatest thing that ever happened to hockey players. Why, the average salaries of the minor leaguers who jumped to the WHA went from $14,000 a year to $30,000. Instead, with all his talk about guarantees he failed to deliver a lot of players to us."

Murphy suspects that there was another factor:

56

Eagleson was doing the negotiating for the Team Canada series with the Russians. He needed the cooperation of the NHL to deliver the bodies.

Despite problems and charges inevitable to a major undertaking, the league was for real and was ready to open for business. Davidson was installed as the first president and Murphy took a franchise, Los Angeles, as part of his finder's fee. Now, players had to be taken to stock these twelve clubs. And many of the men who were going to lay out the money were amateurs in the sports field, fans who were in awe of their own employes. One of the key owners was Jim Cooper of Philadelphia.

"This," says Murphy, "was a case of a successful businessman coming into the sports field—and going wild."

Four

ROBERT G. WOOLF, attorney at law, still can't believe it all. But Woolf, after all, is a man who says "golly" and "hey, wow," and he would be startled if he saw two humming-birds mating. "Imagine," he says, "me, a small-town lawyer from Boston getting all this publicity." Woolf is a man who claims "I've never had a fight with my wife, and when we finally do have one it'll probably be my fault." He is also a man who has handled some of the sports world's most lucrative contracts, and often has received more publicity than his clients. It is simply because he is so engaging. Perhaps guileless is a better word.

The story he tells about his first meeting with Derek Sanderson goes like this: Derek walks unannounced into his office and tells him, "My name is Derek Sanderson, and I'm going to be the world's most famous hockey player." Meanwhile, another of Woolf's private collection of sports flakes, Ken (Hawk) Harrelson of the

58

Boston Red Sox, is in the next room. Woolf summons Harrelson in by saying, "Hawk, I want you to meet your equal."

Harrelson vaulted Woolf onto the sports page one day by announcing he was quitting baseball rather than be traded to Cleveland. The "quitting" was Woolf's idea, and like all great inventions this one made Harrelson and Woolf famous. Finally, Harrelson went to Cleveland for a six-figure contract and the grateful commissioner of baseball, Bowie Kuhn, insisted that Woolf be present at the contract signing. Woolf's picture was flashed all over North America, prominently alongside Harrelson and Kuhn. Woolf's career was ascending. Soon, he gave up his general law practice and devoted himself exclusively to being a "sports attorney." There were lectures at Harvard Law School, national stories, and a growing list of clients. Within two years, Woolf had more than 200 athletes. Strange that he would have a special fondness for Derek, but perhaps no stranger than the fact that old man Adams also was paternal toward the irascible hockey player. There was one similarity between Sanderson and Harrelson, and one that a behavorial psychologist or psychiatrist could spend some time on. Shortly after Harrelson signed his lucrative contract with the Indians, he was on a flight with Woolf. The trip was bumpy and Harrelson broke into a cold sweat and said to Woolf. "We're going to crash. I know it. It's all too good to be true."

Woolf nurtured Sanderson's career, putting Derek on an allowance, paying his parking tickets, questioning his clothing expenditures. Derek was doing pretty well. What with the Stanley Cup money in 1972, the bars, the endorsements, and the $50,000 salary, he was into six figures. Much of the money was working for him in corporate bonds and other conservative issues.

Woolf's career was soaring, too. Who else but the good-natured attorney would wind up representing a coach after heavy negotiations with management over a player's salary. Yet, Woolf represented Harry Sinden, who had left the Bruins in 1970, after the first Stanley Cup, when the club didn't want to pay him more than $20,000. Woolf also became the attorney for Milt Schmidt, the general manager of the Bruins. Doors opened to Woolf that were never opened to an athlete's representative before. Sam Pollock, the genius general manager of the Montreal Canadiens, had always refused to negotiate with a lawyer over one of his players. He talked to Woolf, though. Another executive who had kept his distance from lawyers was Red Auerbach of the Boston Celtics. He, too, met with Woolf and the pair became friends, especially after Woolf convinced the Celtics' John Havlicek to turn down a $1.2 million offer to jump to the American Basketball Association. Ironically, Woolf turned out to be one of the two final candidates for the ABA commissioner's job.

Like everyone else in hockey, Woolf had heard about the creation of the World Association. Derek and some teammates had discussed it, too. It wasn't on his mind, though, in the dressing room as the players tossed around the replica of the Stanley Cup, sipping champagne from it after just defeating the Rangers. Then Weston Adams, Jr., who now held the title of club president, walked over to Sanderson and told him that they would soon discuss a new contract.

A few weeks later, a Miami construction figure named Herb Martin called Woolf. Martin was going to be the head of the Miami Screaming Eagles of the WHA and he told Woolf he wanted Derek. Woolf invited Martin up to Boston.

Martin had already made a mini-name for himself in sports by announcing he was building a 14,000-seat arena in Miami and had already lured the Maple Leafs' goalie, Bernie Parent, to jump for a $600,000, five-year deal. At the time, the $120,000 a year offer to Parent was practically unheard of. Orr and Esposito had signed in midseason with the Bruins. Both were in multi-year deals for six figures a year, but they, after all, were the greatest scoring threats in the history of hockey.

At the end of a lengthy conversation with Woolf, Martin finally said "okay." During the talks Woolf had told Martin that Derek needed $250,000 a year to jump. Martin agreed and offered $2.5 million for ten years. "Okay, that sounds pretty reasonable," Woolf told him. "We'll talk it over."

Woolf then did some checking "to see if he had the money." He met Martin fourteen times, and saw the arena that was halfway up. Martin did have money, but he never would come up with guarantees or personal statements of wealth. Woolf began investigating the other owners. He was impressed that most of them had considerable wealth and weren't simply quick-buck operators. He also dealt with the coach of the New England Whalers, Jack Kelley, and delivered several players to Kelley. "I started to get a little more confident this new league was for real," says Woolf.

But the Screaming Eagles lost their franchise when Martin was unable to put up the other half of the building. This failure, according to Woolf, "left a bitter taste in my mouth and I dismissed the WHA for the time being as not right for Derek."

Woolf at no time, however, worried about the reserve clause, that controversial paragraph that essentially bound a player to his NHL team for life. In effect, the clause read that a player was bound to play for the team the year after the contract expired, even if a salary couldn't be agreed upon. It was a perpetual clause, automatically renewable. It differed from football's option clause, in which a player could be a free agent if he simply played one more year for the team after his contract was up. No one had ever bothered to test whether hockey's reserve clause was valid. Since Derek wasn't under any contractual obligation to the Bruins after the 1971–72 season (except for the reserve clause) Woolf was convinced and "never for a moment doubted" that Derek could jump legally.

In any event, Miami was dead. Long live Philadelphia. The Screaming Eagles franchise had been shifted to the City of Brotherly Love. One day Cooper, the Atlantic City lawyer, called Woolf. He spoke about Derek and how much he admired him. "I want Derek," said Cooper.

Woolf was a little leery. Perhaps to show good faith, Cooper came up with an extraordinary offer for another of Woolf's clients, a minor leaguer named Ron Plumb who was earning $10,000 a year in the Bruins' chain. Cooper offered Plumb a three-year deal worth $195,000—six times Plumb's current salary. That deal was worked out easily enough and Plumb became a Blazer, the new team's nickname.

Now the rumors began that Derek Sanderson would jump to the Blazers. Woolf met with Cooper, but kept the details hidden from Derek. He doesn't like to bother his star client until he can put a package on the table. Derek isn't much for details and his attention span in listening to offers would drive a kindergarten teacher crazy.

Derek knew something was up, though. Still, for

some reason he can't explain he went by himself to see Weston Adams, Jr., known as Westy.

"I figured the WHA was dead after the Miami deal fell through," explains Derek. "So me, big shot, figures he can talk to Westy by himself, without Woolf's help. I told Westy I wanted this on a personal level, just me and him. I knew that he never liked to discuss money with the players. Hell, he's only in his twenties, he's the same age as most of us and he wanted to keep a personal rapport with us. He knew that once he talked money, friendship goes out the window."

Derek went on to tell Adams that he wanted a one-year, no-cut contract. "After I was rid of the first three-year deal that tied me up, all my contracts were for a year," says Derek. "The reason was simple. I never wanted to play exhibition games. So I always held out when I was in training camp. They thought it was for money. But it was always so I could beat the exhibition games tour, so I wouldn't have to go to Halifax and take planes and buses. I'd stay back at our camp in London, Ontario, while the guys were traveling and I'd have a few beers. Everyone always thought I was a prima donna. But I just didn't want to play exhibitions."

Adams, of course, knew about the WHA rumors. He offered Sanderson $80,000 a year for five years—a $400,000 package. Actually, with bonuses for goals-scoring "that I would have picked up as easily as breaking sticks" Derek stood to make at least $100,000 a year. But Westy couldn't offer Derek a no-cut contract in writing. "You'll have to take my word for it," he said. "It's against league rules to have a no-cut contract."

While Derek was talking contract with Adams, Gerry Cheevers, the Bruins' goalie, was talking contract with the WHA. So was John McKenzie, a pugnacious little right wing. Cheevers had just finished a season in which he established a record by going thirty-three straight games without a loss. The club knew it could win with Cheevers in the nets, especially in the clutch games. McKenzie was a sixty-nine point man, a gritty cowpuncher who often would set the tempo for a bruising game by taking a run at an opponent much larger than he was.

But the Bruins were supremely confident they'd keep these players. They didn't think it was necessary to even come close to matching the offers the WHA allegedly made. Who could possibly think of jumping from the NHL, the best of all possible worlds? There was also another factor. A gentlemen's agreement existed in the league that it would not be caught in a bidding war. That is why Parent was able to jump. The Maple Leafs were not going to attempt to match his demands. No one was going to use the WHA as a wedge to get inflated salaries out of the NHL.

The Bruins' dynasty fell apart one night in June, on the eve of the expansion draft.

Derek was driving home from a day of golf when he heard that McKenzie was left "unprotected." This meant that McKenzie could be drafted by either of the two new expansion teams, the New York Islanders or the Atlanta Flames.

"I've got to do something about this," thought Sanderson. "McKenzie's too valuable to the club, he's a team guy and they're underestimating his value in the locker room."

Sanderson immediately called Montreal, where the meetings were staged. He reached Westy, Jr.

"Westy, for crying out loud, what did you do?" asked Sanderson.

"I didn't do anything," the young Adams replied.

"Why are you going to leave McKenzie unprotected in the draft? That's the worst thing you can do. We can't afford to lose him."

Adams explained that McKenzie had only one or two good years left, and the Bruins wanted to protect Ed Westfall, who was younger. Sanderson then inadvertently helped sow the seeds for the Bruins' downfall. He advised Adams to make a deal with Atlanta. The Flames would take Dan Bouchard, the most highly regarded goalie in the Bruins' chain, and the Bruins could then protect McKenzie. "Just keep him in Boston," was Derek's advice. Adams wondered whether the rest of the Bruins felt as strongly about McKenzie, and Derek assured him they did.

"Okay, we'll protect him as long as you can promise me he'll stay."

"Of course he'll stay," Sanderson replied.

In a few days the debacle was over. The Bruins left Westfall unprotected, and he was snatched away. They protected Cheevers and Bouchard was drafted. They didn't protect McKenzie in the first round, but did in the second round.

According to Derek, "After they left McKenzie unprotected, he was so hurt he called his attorney and told him to get in touch with the Blazers. They had offered him $150,000 a year to play and coach."

Westy soon called Derek: "We leave Eddie Westfall unprotected and he's gone. Then we leave McKenzie unprotected, then protect, but he jumps. All because of you." And Westy also knew that Cheevers was contemplating jumping and that Derek was being spoken to.

"I told Westy that I was sorry it happened, but tried

to explain to him that he had hurt Johnny's feelings."

Soon, Cheevers jumped to Cleveland and the Bruins found themselves without some pretty good hockey players. Then McKenzie went to work on Sanderson, trying to convince him to jump, too. "I think that maybe he wanted to get back at the Bruins," says Derek. "He told me that I should do him a favor, and just listen to what Cooper has to say."

Derek claims he still didn't want to leave Boston, but the pressures began to mount. He heard that Storer Broadcasting was negotiating to buy the Bruins and confronted Westy.

"How could you guarantee I'll be in Boston for five years if you're putting the Bruins up for sale?" he asked.

"The Bruins are always up for sale, there's always a possible buyer," Adams explained.

Woolf attempted to calm Derek and told him to take off for Europe. "I put $10,000 in fifties and hundreds into a suitcase and took off the next day," relates Derek.

While Derek was running around across the Atlantic, Cooper came back to Woolf again. He insisted on coming to Boston along with McKenzie to meet Woolf and Derek. Woolf, however, didn't know just where in Europe his client was.

"Okay, me and you—we'll fly to Europe and find him," replied Cooper.

Cooper then invited Woolf down to Philadelphia. "We'll talk," said Woolf. "But you'll have to make him the highest paid athlete in the world, or else Derek wouldn't be interested."

Woolf spent many sleepless nights going over the contract and thinking of reasons why Derek shouldn't go. In Boston he was a hero, transcending generation and socioeconomic gaps. His big money was starting. He was well regarded and he had a fame that ranked him near the top of his profession. He also was playing for the most successful league in sports history, where 90 percent of the seats were sold. It had a tradition and a marketable name.

One night Woolf awoke. "They'll never go for this," he exclaimed. He had decided to put Harold Sanderson on the payroll at $25,000 a year. For four years.

Another sleepless night. "Up front money," thought Woolf. "I'll ask for half a million dollars for the first year —no matter what. Even if the league folds, if the reserve clause is upheld by the Supreme Court and the Bruins get him back—no matter what, Derek will get half a million in cash."

Woolf later recalled, "The contract had to be perfect. If it wasn't it would be worthless. If there were escape clauses in it, if the Blazers didn't make money, if the deal fell through, then Derek would look bad. He'd be a man without a country, so to speak. Whatever happened, he couldn't be embarrassed. Even if there was an injunction and he couldn't play, he'd have to get paid. He was taking an awful big chance, after all, and I had to make sure he'd come out of it okay. I guess it was like performing an operation. The whole procedure had to be perfect or the patient would die."

More talks followed with Cooper. At one point Cooper said, "But these sums are unheard of," and Woolf replied, "I know that. But it's the only way you'll appeal to Derek." Each outlandish request ultimately was approved by Cooper. Finally, the deal was hammered out.

Essentially, it called for the $2.65 million to be spread over ten years. That sum included the $100,000 his father would receive, so perhaps that amount should be deducted from the contract. However, the deal actually could have been worth more. There were bonus provisions based on goal figures. If Derek, for example, reached the thirty-goal plateau, he'd receive an extra few thousand dollars. If he got forty goals there'd be even more money—each and every year. But say, for example, that Derek wanted to retire after five years. That was okay, too. He'd be a scout for $100,000 a year for the next five years.

The final hammering out virtually doubled Cooper's original offer. Woolf had made as much of an issue of such intangibles as Derek's "charisma factor" and gate appeal as his very real talents. Derek was a man around whom to build a franchise.

"Everyone said that Bobby Orr was the only hockey player who could bring people into a building," relates Derek. "But the way I see it is like this. It's like people going to see a great singer perform. But you need something between the acts. I'd be the stripper between the acts. I'd be brought in to entertain the nuts in the group."

The offer was put on the table. Derek spoke about not having any friends in Philadelphia. He also was concerned about places to hang out. "Where can I go there?" he asked.

"Buy your own place," Cooper answered.

Along with Woolf and Derek and Cooper at the meeting were Derek's business partners in the bars— McDonough and Cimino.

McDonough whispered to Derek: "I don't believe it. Two and a half million dollars. It's like Michael Anthony on that old television show 'The Millionaire.'"

Derek remained worried and told Cooper he would have to think about it.

"Think about it?" Cooper exclaimed. "You're twenty-six years old and you have to think about two and a half million dollars?"

But there were things to think about, of course. Some quick thoughts flashed through Sanderson's mind: the other deals he'd been offered in the past. One was for go-karts. Another man wanted him to invest $15,000 in a white rat ranch in Wyoming.

Before anything else, though, Woolf and Sanderson felt they had to go back to talk to the old man— Weston Adams, Sr. A battle plan had to be worked out, Sanderson believed. Truly, this was an offer he couldn't refuse, and so he decided to take to the mattresses before confronting the patriarch.

"We holed up for three days," explains Derek. "I didn't want to be disturbed. Cooper, though, wanted an immediate answer. He wanted to start the season's ticket sales to rolling, and he wanted to advertise me."

Cooper had wanted to sign Derek within three days "or the deal would be off." Jimmy Cimino told Cooper, though, that "we need seven banking days."

Sanderson wondered what Cimino was trying to do. Was there some business deal cooking that the three partners had to work out? "No," Cimino explained. "We've got to give us some time to talk this out."

At the apartment Cimino said, "Okay, let's do this scientifically." He got out some graph paper. He put an X on the bottom of the paper and said, "Okay, here's where we are." Then he put "$2.65 million" on the top. "That's what we can get," Cimino explained.

"There is a law of diminishing returns," Cimino told Derek. "Everything you have going for you right now is a plus. The people are behind you. The press is behind you. The money is there. The Bruins haven't said anything bad about you and you haven't knocked them. You haven't seen a negative. So we don't move until we see that negative that can square the deal. Then we move. The first time someone pulls back an inch, or a bad story appears about you, or someone raps you on television, then you got to make a move. That's when you make your stand, before you lose it."

They started to plot what the money could mean. "Hey, when people find out you're worth almost $3 million, the bank would give you a note for $4 million and you could build a hotel," Cimino advised.

"I didn't have Bob Woolf along while we were throwing out all these ideas," concedes Derek, "because I underestimated Bob and his friendship. I see now that all he wanted was what's best for me. He's very security conscious. Future and security. He kept telling me that I could take care of my parents first. Above all else they must salt it away."

But Derek only spoke to Woolf in the afternoons, after the phone calls would come in from newsmen who heard rumors. It wasn't so much that Derek didn't want financial advice from Woolf at this point. It was simply that he had supreme trust and faith in Cimino and Mc-Donough. The three of them had left Bachelors III and struck out on their own when they started the singles bars. Now there were three places—Daisy Buchanan, Zelda's, and Gatsby's.

"Don't worry about us," Cimino told Derek. "We can always make some lunch money. Maybe we'll go into business in Philadelphia."

More advice followed. "Let's give the Bruins every opportunity," said Woolf. "We cannot leave this city with any rancor. Keep your mouth shut and don't say anything bad about the Boston Bruins."

By the end of the third day, after all the talking and planning, McDonough finally asked, "Here's what it boils down to. Would you be happy in Philadelphia?"

"I finally went onto the streets after three days," says Derek. "People came up to me, shaking my hand. 'You got to take the money,' they told me. Lunch-bucket workers, Italians from the North End. All of them, 'Hey, Turkey, good luck. Give me a loan if you don't know what to do with the dough.' The man in the street—he never said don't go. He said come back and say hello to us sometime."

The Bruins by now had reached Sanderson, and Derek believes they had used secretaries to try to track him down. "They'd have a girl call my room, and when McDonough or Cimino answered she'd say she was a friend of mine, hoping they'd put the call through. But they didn't fall for it."

Young Adams did reach Woolf, though, and they all agreed to go out to dinner. Westy pulled up in a chauffeur-driven limousine and Cimino winced. He told Derek, "It's a power play. They're trying to impress you, put you off guard." Derek remembers that it was a rented limousine, quite unusual for a casual drive. "God love Westy. He's beautiful," says Derek charitably.

"We had an uneasy conversation in the back of the car," recalls Derek. "How you doing? Great. Golfing? Yeah." Then Derek asked Westy how things were. "I got a lot of problems these days," said young Adams. "My golf's not too good. You're cutting into my vacation."

At the restaurant, they were ushered into a private room and Westy turned to the waiter and said, "That will be all, Charles." The door was closed. "You promised me McKenzie and he's gone. We lost Westfall. We lost Cheevers. Now you're going to jump. You're destroying the franchise. There's no loyalty in your bones."

"What the hell are you talking about?" Derek demanded. "You're going to sell the club."

"It's a family business," explained Adams. "You can't fight the power structure with family money."

"But New York's signing guys for 200 grand," Sanderson told him. "They want to keep their guys. They're going to try to buy the Stanley Cup."

"I know," replied Westy. "But they're a big conglomerate. We can't do it. A wage war can destroy us. We simply can't afford it."

Westy knew Derek loved his father. The old man was dying of cancer, and Derek knew that, too. Westy said, "Dad wants to see you. He's not feeling too well. He's out in Marblehead. You want to come over and talk to him?"

Sanderson called Cimino and told him of the talk and the fact he had agreed to meet with the old man. "And he's liable to persuade me to stay in Boston," said Sanderson. "Don't break," said Cimino. "Don't let Westy use the old man trick on you."

But Derek also called Woolf, who advised him, "We owe it to Mr. Adams and the Bruins to meet with them."

Woolf, Sanderson, Cimino, and McDonough went to Marblehead. On the way over, Woolf asked Derek, "How close do you want the Bruins to get?" "Reasonably," replied Derek. "How reasonable?" Derek answered, "$125,000 a year."

"I would have stayed in Boston for that, but no one will believe that," says Derek. "Even Woolf and Cimino and McDonough, they didn't believe when I said that— that I'd give up 400 grand."

One of his partners turned to him and said, "I know you love the old man, Derek. But remember, this is business. Strictly business. You have a talent and Philadephia wants it. They want it five times more than the

Bruins want it. Remember, if Boston had the right deal they'd trade you tomorrow."

Sanderson replied, "They could have traded me. I could have gone to the Rangers for Tkaczuk and Seiling, but the Bruins kept me around. I wouldn't have this image, this name, this reputation, if it weren't for Boston. Everything I have I owe to Boston. They allowed me to say what I wanted to say. They allowed me to dress the way I wanted to dress—the white skates, the long hair, the mustache. A lot of clubs wouldn't have allowed me to do it."

The lawyer replied: "You also put a lot of people in the building."

So they met the old man. Derek remembers it this way: "He comes to the door with his cane and his old Yankee outfit. You know, the white cotton shirt, cuff pants, brogue shoes. He cleared his throat and said, 'You've been causing me a lot of trouble.' I said I knew that, and I laughed. And he said, 'Okay, let's have a couple of drinks and discuss this.'"

The drinks made both principals wistful. "You've got a beautiful home, Mr. Adams," said Derek.

"Well, I'm getting old. I like the harbor and the ocean. I like my peace." (He was dead within 200 days.) He continued: "I'm really too old. I'm out of this business now, you know. Chairman of the board. I'm retired. But there's problems coming up all the time, problems, problems. I have no stock, no say, really." Westy interrupted him. "Yeah, dad, I'd like to have your stock and your say." Sanderson chuckled and said, "Hey, someone's not exactly telling the truth around here." The old man said, "Oh, well, they pay attention to me, sure." And then his voice rose.

"What are you trying to do to me?" he asked Sanderson.

"I'm not trying to do anything to you," replied Derek. "Someone gave me an offer of two and a half million dollars. My old man caged a lunch bucket all his life, you know."

Soon they were screaming, a "good old fashioned Harvard scream," relates Derek, as they got into the morals of the issue.

"Don't talk to me about morals," said the player. "How many guys did hockey bury because it didn't like the way they talked? Or looked? Or they had two beers too many? Sure, hockey's given a lot of players great opportunities and great lives, but it also hurt a lot by burying them in the minors because it didn't want someone else to have them, or it didn't like them. Hockey treated a player like he was a piece of meat, like he was cattle.

"They didn't worry about a guy's home, his kid's education, his friends. Trade him. If they don't produce, get rid of him. It's about time the players started getting even."

The old man interrupted briefly to point out that "if it wasn't for the National Hockey League, you wouldn't be here." But Derek couldn't be stopped. He was on his own ground now. For he was, ultimately, a piece of meat and he knew what that felt like. He had had enough of "Harvard intellectuals" (his words) putting him down because he sweated for a living, and he was tired of playing games at parties where he had to impress someone by giving a lecture on Greek mythology. "What do you know about a Pyrrhic victory?" he had once been asked. And he proceeded to explain who King Pyrrhus was. He had enjoyed to some degree these sudden outbursts of culture when he'd enchant some liberal friends with discourses on Euripides. But there was almost something defensive about the fact that he had to bring up these esoteric names to prove he simply wasn't another jock. Now he said to old man Adams, "I know what the National League has done for me. But I'm a saleable commodity and I'm here as a businessman and I'm going to sell myself to the highest bidder."

"Where's your loyalty," screamed Adams. "Where's your character? I always thought you had character. You're selling yourself for money." Sanderson answered, "You're in the stock market every day. You buy and sell your money. I can't do that. I've got to sell myself."

Adams became paternal. "Look, I want to tell you about these rogues, these thieves . . . ." Sanderson was impressed by the fact that the old man never swore. Instead he used words that would make a country gentleman's blood boil—"rogues, thieves." He never even mentioned the WHA by name. "Careful, Mr. Adams, watch your heart, don't get excited," Derek advised him.

"Screw my heart," shouted Adams.

"It's like thieves were walking into my home. And I've got antiques and beautiful paintings. They walk in and take my best paintings off the wall and give me a token amount of money. I worked all these years, sweated and worried and got ulcers. This team has been my whole life. It's all I've got left now. You're helping to take all this away from me. These thieves, these upstarts, these vandals—how can they come in and take my life away from me? There's no justice in America if the courts decide otherwise." He shook his cane toward heaven.

Sanderson wavered. "I really felt for the man. But I told him that there's no justice in America if the courts allow a monopoly. And I told him that if it comes to a court case, things would go bad for him and his league. He refused to believe this. He said he'd leave the case in the hands of the courts, that men wouldn't be judges if they weren't fair men. He really believed that his position was honorable. He was, I guess, a very trusting man who believed in the rightness of what he'd done and that the courts and the American way would back him up. And I saw this side of him, really a good side. I mean, if a man really believes in his position, and he's willing to suffer losses for that position, then you must respect him."

Images flashed through Derek's mind while the old man was talking. He remembered how the Bruins had played badly against the Rangers the opening game of the season, and how the old man had called him up after the game and told him, "Derek, I want you to play the way I know you can play." And three days later the Bruins routed the Rangers and Sanderson starred and he got another phone call. This time the old man said, "That's the way. Only 76 games left." He remembered when Harry Sinden and Milt Schmidt were contemplating trading him but the old man turned it down. There was always a pleasant nod from Adams, always a "Hi, how are you?"

Sanderson was brought back to reality. "We've been friends a long time," said Adams. "Let's figure out what's best for both of us. I just want you to understand how I feel. I don't want to lose you. You're my boy and you've been my boy since you were 15. I watched you grow up, I watched you play well. I've always pulled for you."

"I know, and I owe you for that," replied Derek. "All I want you to do is to come reasonably close. I don't want to leave."

"Well, how close is reasonable." asked Adams.

"Let's leave that to the negotiators," Sanderson answered, looking at Woolf and Charles Mulcahy, the

Bruins' counsel who signed the players. "Is the deal legitimate with Philadelphia?" Adams asked. "Is the money up front?" Woolf replied, "Yes it is, Mr. Adams." Adams said, "All that money, eh, son? That's a lot of money. I guess you've got only a few short years to earn your money."

Adams's tone was changing, and it was apparent that he realized that he was going to lose the man he referred to as "Sandy." "Much as I don't want to see you go—as an owner I hate you for it—but as a friend, you've got to take it. Go with my blessings. I can't enter a wage war. I hope you understand that. It's important that you do. Okay, we'll let the big shot attorneys and negotiators handle it," he concluded, and Derek knew that it was over. "Let's have a beer while the others go into the other room and talk about it," said the old man.

"I knew it was just a formality from then on," Sanderson was to recall. "Oh, they spoke about a loan, interest-free, for $1 million, things like that. But the meeting was over, and Woolf came over to me and said, 'God love him, the man believes he's right and you can't knock a man who believes he's right. He's a gentleman and let's leave the door open.'"

Everyone shook hands. A few days later Derek called Adams. He asked if there was any change and the old man replied there wasn't. That was that. But the old man said, "Call once in a while, let me know how you're doing. Get good financial advice. We're going to miss you, you little rascal. I used to like watching you running around, hitting the odd guy. I'm going to miss that."

Derek told him that if he didn't hear from him in forty-eight hours he was going to Philadelphia.

"And I left. I flew to Philadelphia and I signed."

Five

THE WHA spurred the greatest, most outlandish money war in sports history. There had been some publicized contracts in basketball, but only a few names actually benefitted from that tussle, and they were rookies who had options on which league to join. But for the first time, a major sports league's entry involved the established stars to a significant degree. When one realizes that in 1970, for example, the average NHL player received $22,000 a year, and that two years later his average was $44,000—then the impact of the WHA can be measured. And everyone, it seemed, wanted a piece of the action.

There was, for example, that shadowy figure who was to become known as "the Merchant of Vienna." He "looked like Kurt Kaszner and spoke like Peter Lorre," recalls one club official. The Merchant had become famous—or infamous—as a European super scout in the late 1960s, when two North American soccer leagues were formed. However, few people in either Canada or the United States knew much about soccer, especially on the management level. The Merchant had presented himself as one of the world's great authorities. He was going to scour Europe and bring back the top players. Owners had never heard the names of anyone who played soccer, and the Merchant said he could deliver the best. So when he plucked second-line players from Division III teams, who was to know Division III meant that, in ability, they ranked behind divisions I and II? In addition, the Merchant made money three ways: He got a finder's fee from the soccer teams in North America for finding the player, an agent's fee from the player, and another fee from the club that sold the player. Now there was another fertile field—hockey. "I can get you players from the Soviet Union," said the Merchant in his best conspiratorial, Peter Lorre voice. He told the owners that he could bring over most players for only $16,000; it would cost the team $9,000 a year in salary, and $7,000 would go to the Merchant. That seemed fair enough, and the league bankrolled him.

Apparently, he told a different story to the European players he tried to entice across the sea. Ulf Sterner, a Swede who had a brief fling in the NHL, was promised $35,000 a year by the Merchant if he came back to the United States. The Chicago Cougars, in fact, thought they had signed Sterner only to discover the contract was a forgery. No European players were imported, and no one defected from the Soviet Union.

That meant all the players in the WHA had to come from the existing pool of talent in North America. And people already had been complaining that the

14-team NHL—with a total of only about 280 players —was watered down from expansion. So it became a players' market, and some of them acted rather less than chivalrous. "The players," said one executive, "became like the owners used to be. The pendulum had swung the other way."

Item: One NHL star was offered $100,000 a year (a $40,000 raise) to jump. To show good faith, the WHA club gave him a $50,000 advance. But then the new club didn't come up with the remaining guarantee by the specified date. The player kept the money, on advice of his attorney. "It'll cost them $100,000 to get back the $50,000," he told his client.

Item: An American League journeyman was signed by a WHA team and received a $2,000 bonus, another $1,000 for expenses to report to camp early, and meal money. The day before camp opened he jumped back to his American League club. He never returned any of the money. "We'll get it back in court," the owner said. The owner subsequently quit, too.

Item: At a big news conference in New York, Cowboy Bill Flett jumped from the Philadelphia Flyers to the Raiders. A few days later he was gone. He had jumped back to the Flyers despite signing a Raider contract. He will receive triple his previous year's salary, and there are rumors he also got $100,000 as a bonus for his astuteness in seeing the light.

Item: Ron Ward, who scored two goals with the Vancouver Canucks and received $18,000, was signed by the Raiders for $40,000. (When the season ended he wanted his contract torn up and demanded $100,000 annually.)

But the really big news started to make the headlines when the really big stars were wooed. After Parent, the big one to make the move was Bobby Hull, the Golden Jet of the Chicago Black Hawks who has had some of history's strangest negotiations—with Chicago and the team he left for, the Winnipeg Jets. Hull, perhaps more than anyone, gave credibility to the new league. Once he signed, not only did others follow, but also he helped jack up the price of those who stayed.

He was probably the most appealing player in hockey's new era, a heavily muscled, soft-spoken Adonis who thought nothing of spending forty-five minutes after a game—and holding up the plane charter—to sign autographs. His 604 goals made him the highest active goal-scorer in the NHL and even though his thinning hair required transplants, he was still a commanding figure. He had just scored fifty goals, giving him a record five fifty-goal seasons.

Yet, he had reached the $100,000 plateau only a year before. He had undergone a series of celebrated rifts with management, despite his superstar status. He was, without doubt, the most attractive forward in hockey—perhaps in the sport's history. In his hand the curved stick had become a weapon of awesome proportions and the slap shot he popularized turned the game into the booming sport it has become. But his money difficulties, including problems with a huge cattle-breeding ranch, didn't quite make him the millionaire he had hoped to be. Some of his money wars with management were comic-opera. There was, for example, the alleged $100,000 contract with Jim Norris, the late owner of the Hawks. Shortly before Norris died, according to Hull's agent at the time, Norris and Hull had agreed to hockey's first $100,000 contract. The deal was, we are asked to believe, written in pencil on a sheet of yellow note paper. No copies were made and Hull stuffed the paper in a jacket pocket. According to the agent, "Bobby took a cab ride and had the paper with him. When he left the cab, the paper was gone."

Norris died. Management denied any such piece of paper existed. Both sides called each other liars. Why a hockey player who had gone through hell in previous negotiations had only a lined, yellow piece of paper to prove a $100,000 deal was never explained. And if the deal in fact was made, who could believe that Norris, one of the world's wealthiest men, would not have such a deal witnessed?

A new deal was made, but not for $100,000. As part of the agreement Hull was required to apologize to his team and fans for holding out over the paper. This he did. He blamed "poor advice." Soon he had a new agent, a Chicago CPA named Harvey Wineberg, whose only other sports client was the tempestuous Leo Durocher.

Wineberg was amused when Ben Hatskin approached him and started talking about millions of dollars. "I couldn't imagine Bobby getting involved," says Wineberg. "I couldn't see him picking up after fifteen years with only a few more to play. At that point in his life the Black Hawks had sort of inferred they'd take care of Bobby when his playing career was over. I thought the WHA was a nice thing, but I couldn't get excited over it."

Hatskin persisted. He began talking outrageous figures, sums that had never before been mentioned in the same breath with hockey players. Hockey was a sport, after all, in which the Rangers' leading scorer earned less money than a substitute on the Knickerbockers' basketball team. Perhaps Hatskin growled and yelled and pushed, emotional displays he is proud of. In any event, Wineberg and Hull listened. The talk got higher and higher and one day they all agreed to the following: Hull would receive a ten-year deal worth $1.75 million—for the first five years he would receive $250,000 annually as player-coach, and then $100,000 a year for the remaining five as coach. But there was more—$1 million in cash.

That was the big one. Unbelievable as it seemed, Bobby would get a check for that extraordinary figure. Even if he was enjoined from playing, even if he never suited up for a WHA game, he was to keep that bonus for signing the contract. With Hull signing, a cover of legitimacy had been put over the infant league, born out of wedlock.

In a deal of such magnitude that it had to be consummated in two countries, Hull officially jumped by first taking his check for $1 million in St. Paul, and then flying by charter to Winnipeg where, on Portage and Main streets, he signed the ten-year contract. In a sense, the $1 million was an advance against royalties. It was put up by the league's properties division, which handled endorsements. The first $1 million of royalties on Hull-endorsed products (which would require sales of about $20-million to repay) would be returned to the WHA. This $1 million check was made possible after the twelve clubs each contributed money, some putting up more, some less. In a sense, then, Bobby Hull was a group investment and each member of the league knew full well that he was critical to their success.

Immediately, the $1 million was put in a bank, where it began to earn $1,000 a week interest. There were good reasons for accepting the money in cash, not all of them understood by the majority of fans. First, the maximum tax on "earned income" (salary) for that year was only 50 percent. In other words, at the outside Hull could be taxed only $500,000. Who knew what the taxes would be like in the future? And with all the tax shelters available, it was likely that Hull's actual income tax would amount to much less than half. The reason, too, that the $1 million was presented in the States was to take advantage of this relatively low tax. In Canada, it would have amounted to about 70 percent. Players started to see green.

There is another group of people interested in money—organized crime. And one day, across Canada, pictures appeared of a short stocky man who said he was Joe Columbo, Jr., and was buying a house in Winnipeg to be near his investment in a hockey club.

It didn't seem at first all that unusual that Columbo would be moving to Canada from New York. His father, a reputed Mafia boss, had been shot in the head during Italian-American Day festivities near Central Park. Why not escape future danger by moving into a nice residential area of Winnipeg?

When Columbo was called and asked why he was moving to Canada, he didn't know what people were talking about. He wasn't moving anywhere, he said. Then the picture in the paper was compared to other pictures of Columbo. The man in Canada was a fraud.

Some WHA members believed the whole thing was an NHL plot to discredit Hatskin and the league. It wasn't. The man who played Columbo had a history of impersonating famous personages. Now he simply was extending his routine to include the Mafia.

By this time Jim Cooper had been in heavy negotiations with Derek and Woolf, even though Cooper had been a franchise holder for only a matter of weeks. Cooper had been a hockey fan and had secretly dreamed that one day he would own a franchise. He had even, a few years earlier, discussed the possibility of reviving with Bernie Brown the Jersey Seagulls of the Eastern League.

Through one of those lucky (or unlucky) accidents of time and place, Cooper became a WHA owner. Leaving a convention of trial lawyers he came across Dick Wood, another lawyer and president of the New York Raiders. He told Wood that it wouldn't be a bad idea if Philadelphia could come up with a franchise in the new league. Wood told him there was a league meeting the following morning in Quebec, and would Cooper be interested in making a pitch?

Within five hours Cooper raised the money and was en route to Quebec, arriving at the airport before Wood. After he had left Wood to drive home, he had started to figure what all this would cost.

"I thought it would take $4 to $5 million in losses over four years," he says. "Then I phoned Bernie Brown, a fellow whom I had known for a number of years. He was the chairman of one bank, I was the chairman of another bank not far away. Bernie really wasn't too interested in sports, but he knew his kids were. Anyway, we had a ten-minute phone conversation and we agreed on the financing. Most of the money would be his, but we'd be equal partners in the equity of the franchise. I suppose he went into it to give his kids something."

The next morning Cooper was in Quebec and was awarded a franchise. He wrote out a check to the league for $210,000. The price had gone up quite a bit from the original $25,000 franchise fee, but it also included Parent. Thus, within 24 hours Cooper had gone from a successful trial attorney to the president of a hockey club that had one player, in a league that had never sold a seat. But he was happy; in fact, he was ecstatic.

"Then we sat down and figured what we needed," says Cooper. "We wanted important names like Andre Lacroix, John McKenzie, Derek Sanderson. People told us McKenzie wasn't interested, but that some day he would like to manage. I figured why not make some day today, and so we got him. But Derek was the star we needed—it would give an instant identity to a new franchise. In sports and entertainment you need a star quality. Sonny Werblin knew that when he got Joe Namath for the Jets. The difference was that Namath had the chance to play and he became a star. Unfortunately for us and Derek, he never had the chance once he got to us.

"Anyway, the big problem with Derek simply was trying to find him. He was traveling all over the world. After I contacted Bob Woolf, I had to find Derek and tell him we were interested. I got our people to man the phones and we finally located him. It's not as unusual as it sounds. After all, when you run a law office you're always trying to get hold of people who may be running away, or who you need as witnesses."

As seen from Cooper's side, once contact was made "it was necessary that we make an appeal to him he couldn't resist." Cooper knew about Derek's loyalty to Weston Adams, Sr., and for a while it appeared to the fledgling owner that this would prove insurmountable. Cooper knew, too, that he was asking a young player, who had security and fame, to move into a very visible position in a new league, and that if things didn't work out Derek's reputation would be tarnished. "We had to structure the offer so it would be tantalizing—it would appeal to his ego."

Cooper agrees that the package indeed came to about $2.6 million, but he remembers the details a bit differently from Sanderson. Derek, he says, was to receive "only" $400,000 in cash the first year—and $100,000 of that was a loan. "It was partly for tax purposes, partly to make him the world's highest salaried athlete. He liked the way that sounded, that he would make more money than Pele, the soccer star, who he heard was getting about $300,000." For the next year Derek also was to receive $300,000. Then the rest of the money would be distributed to gross Derek between $200,000 to $250,000 a year for the length of the contract. Interestingly, if Derek broke his leg in the first game he still would be paid for four years—about $1 million.

Cooper vividly recalls the moment he discovered that Derek was his. The night that Sanderson had gone up to Marblehead to visit the old man, Cooper and McKenzie went to a Chinese restaurant. Cooper was waiting to call Woolf to find out whether the Bruins had enticed Derek into remaining with Boston. At the end of his meal, Cooper saw four fortune cookies on the table. Two of them read, "Tonight you will make a great business deal." He rushed to a phone, called Woolf, and discovered that Derek was going to become a Blazer. He stuffed the papers from the fortune cookies into his wallet, and carries them to this day.

Okay. Cooper now had the world's highest salaried athlete. He also had a building that could hold about 8,000 people—perhaps 10,000 with standing room. The team would play thirty-nine home games. That meant that approximately $10,000 a game (about 15 percent of the gross receipts) would go to pay Derek's salary.

"We felt that with Derek and other name players we could produce a winner in Philadelphia—which the city hadn't had for years," explains Cooper. "That's why we were doing all this. We figured that with a winner we could bring in 9,000 fans a game. If we could do that, we'd lose only half a million the first year."

Brown wasn't happy about Derek's salary—he was the man who ultimately would have to pay it. Brown then decided that every seat would be raised $1 over the original figure in order to pay Derek. Initially, the top seat was to cost $7.50. Cooper was against the price increase, but it was out of his jurisdiction in the partnership. However, the price was raised to $8.50—more money than the established Flyers of the NHL were charging in the Spectrum. Because of the way the seating was arranged in the Blazers' arena, more than half the seats wound up costing $8.50. Brown isn't a man who takes no for an answer. He was determined to get his way. A former associate says of him, "No one survives in trucking in New Jersey unless you're tough. He went from owning a single coal truck to a fleet of more than 4,000 trailers."

Of course, Cooper couldn't keep running things indefinitely. He needed a hockey man at the helm, a general manager who knew the ropes. He was pleased, therefore, when the popular Murray Williamson, coach of the surprising United States Olympic team, called and asked for the job. It was perfect, believed Cooper. Williamson was young and accustomed to dealing with the new breed of hockey player, who was becoming more sophisticated and more like other young men in North America—with the same rebellions and attitude. Williamson was hired as general manager.

On a Sunday night, the eve of the press conference to announce Williamson's arrival, Williamson went out for a beer with Kevin Johnson, the club's public relations director. The news conference was going to be a major one, but people didn't know exactly what was to be announced. There was no formal organization on the Blazers just yet. Only one man was under contract— Parent. Sanderson still hadn't formally signed. Lacroix had agreed to terms, but his news conference would be scheduled for Wednesday. Johnson didn't want to detract from Williamson's coming.

Johnson and Williamson sat at a bar and Williamson suddenly said, "I don't think I can go through with it."

"Hey, listen, the Philadelphia press is tough, but you'll do okay in the press conference," replied Johnson.

"I don't mean the press conference. I mean the job," Williamson replied.

He went on to explain that the Blazers had joined the league later than anyone else. Except for Parent, no one else had a contract. Johnson, in fact, was the only man drawing a salary. The season would be opening soon and he felt the building job was impossible.

It was now midnight. The press conference was scheduled for 9 o'clock the next morning. After talking to Cooper, Johnson telephoned Lacroix at 2 A.M. and told him to bring his wife and family to the 9 A.M. news conference. And that's what he did. The next morning the Philadelphia press greeted the arrival of Andre Lacroix to their city, never knowing that they originally were called to meet the general manager.

It may well be that a gentleman's agreement existed in the National Hockey League not to bow to salary demands, and not be brought into a wage war. One story goes that the reason the Toronto Maple Leafs allowed Parent to jump was to show the rest of the players the owners wouldn't meet outrageous demands. If there was in fact such an agreement, the Rangers didn't abide by it. They underwent the most radical salary upsurge in professional sports history.

Hull's signing had created a whole different environment. People now knew that these absurd figures that were tossed around had some basis in fact. So when the Rangers' star defenseman, Brad Park, was offered $1 million for four years to jump to Cleveland, or when his teammate, Vic Hadfield, received the same offer, they investigated.

Perhaps the most pragmatic team president in hockey, the Rangers' Bill Jennings, knew that it would take only money to keep his stars. And he agreed to pay them. Thus Park, who had received about $12,000 two years before, was jumped to $200,000 a year for five years. He didn't realize it at the time, but Park became the highest salaried player in the NHL with his leap. Bobby Orr had signed a long-term contract in the middle of the previous season—when the Bruins had heard the faint birth screams of the WHA—and wanted Orr tied up. Orr's contract, however, called for only about $180,000 a year.

Meanwhile, Hadfield, represented by Woolf, also was signed by Francis, after Jennings gave the go-ahead. Hadfield signed a five-year deal worth almost $1 million. Two years earlier, Hadfield had held out for an increase of his $30,000 salary. When Jean Ratelle and Rod Gilbert, Hadfield's linemates, saw how much he was getting they wanted it, too. They got it. Walt Tkaczuk, the hard-nosed center, also got a big boost. While Park had been earning $12,000 a few years before, Tkaczuk was making $14,000. Now he was up in the $130,000 class. These five players alone were to be paid more money than all the Rangers combined had received at the start of the 1971–72 season.

When the payments were over, Jennings said to a friend on the golf course, "Well, I didn't think it could be done, but I think we've bought ourselves the Stanley Cup."

It is difficult for the average sports fan—even the fanatic hockey follower—to appreciate the dramatic turnaround the WHA made in the lives of hockey players.

It gave them an option—to go where they wanted to. Every monopoly—and the NHL was no exception—has its share of excesses. When you know you control the destinies of everyone who works for you, and they had better do it your way or they're gone, you create a dictatorial system. Power corrupts and even though the president of the league, or a general manager of an expansion team, might be the world's nicest person, he is unwittingly part of the power structure that perpetuates itself. Without his realizing it—without, perhaps, malice —he has become a demi-god.

Hockey has been filled with its tyrants, its knaves, as well as its heroes and progressives. But the important thing to remember is that no matter how fine anyone at the top was, he ultimately had things his own way.

Thus, once a youngster became the property of a team in the juniors, his future was in management's hands. If he didn't like playing where he was, if he couldn't get along with an owner, if he had family problems that required him to be home, he could solve these difficulties only by the good graces of the owner. The system was self-protective for the NHL. Players today still remember their colleagues who were "buried" in the minors because the general manager didn't like their attitude, or perhaps the g.m. didn't want to make a trade that conceivably could help a rival.

Phil Esposito remembers an old boyhood friend, Gene Ubriaco, who was buried in the minors because he couldn't get along with management. Ubriaco could have made it earlier to the big leagues. But he was a marginal sort of player, and his club could afford to keep him down—and keep him away from anyone else interested in him. Ubriaco quit the pro ranks rather than remain someone else's property.

Ted Lindsay, a clubhouse lawyer (and great player) for the Detroit Red Wings, was traded to the Chicago Black Hawks after he had complained about injustices in the pension system, and the fact that a player couldn't be his own man. Perhaps it was simply coincidence that the year Lindsay was traded the pension plan was upgraded considerably and the playoff prize money was raised. Later, when Lindsay became a television announcer for the NHL, he slapped Sanderson on the wrist because Sanderson had jumped back to the Bruins. Lindsay, in fact, said the Bruins "were crazy" to take Derek back. The confrontation took place on network television, and Sanderson coolly replied that Lindsay was "on TV now, and had to say something to sound controversial."

It is important to understand one of the underlying fundamentals of hockey: originally it was a game for amateur sportsmen. To get paid to play? Why, no gentleman would even think of it. Even North America's oldest team trophy, the cherished Stanley Cup, was originally donated to go to the best "amateur" team in Canada. That distinction was made. Lord Stanley probably couldn't envision that a professional team would dare to make a bid for it.

Canadians wouldn't even acknowledge that one of their own would play hockey for money. There were no official pro teams in Canada. In fact, the first admitted professional hockey clubs started in the United States in the early 1900s. Americans, perhaps, felt no stigma attached to taking money to play a game. At least, not as much as their brothers north of the border, who had been steeped in traditional British thinking.

The man who owned the first pro team was a dentist named Gibson. He formed a club in Houghton, Michigan, and named it Portage Lakes. Few Americans knew how to play hockey, though. He then started a grand tradition—importing Canadians. Virtually every player on his team was Canadian and they soundly routed all their opposition in small American midwestern towns. Each player he brought in was paid. They might play for a game or two, and then jump back to their more respectable Canadian amateur club. Soon, the world's first professional hockey league was formed. It was called the International Pro Hockey League and contained only American teams—with Canadian players.

It took a few years, but finally a Canadian team, from Sault Ste. Marie, admitted it was a professional squad. Then an actual Canadian league was formed with play-for-pay boys, the Ontario Professional Hockey League. It was now 1908—fifteen years after the Stanley Cup had been donated. Because the owners had to pay money to their players management decided that a change was in order. Before, hockey had been a seven-man game. That was okay. The people who ran the club made money and didn't have to pay the players. Amateurism was okay for the players—but not the owners. Once players started receiving money, though, a rule change was required: cut the number of players on a team to six. Less mouths to feed. That is why there is six-man hockey today.

The first player revolt began in 1915, soon after the National Hockey Association was formed. Ironically, it was started by a man who was to become one of the bulwarks of the Bruins as general manager—Art Ross. His name is so respected in NHL circles these days that the trophy bearing his name goes to the league's leading scorer. In those days, however, he was on the other side of the fence. He was angry when his club put a ceiling of $6,000 on salaries for the whole team. Since he alone had earned almost $3,000 the previous season, he realized that he would have to take a cut in pay. So he did what seemed only logical at the time; he threatened to start a rival league. For his big mouth he was suspended by the NHA. The league quickly reconsidered, however, after Ross showed that he was serious and really was going to go into business against the Establishment. He was welcomed back.

In those early years, loyalty was a matter of definition. Players often jumped back and forth between teams, going to the highest bidder. Most players were under one-year contracts and the others had no formal deals.

And then it happened. A rival league was formed—on the Pacific coast of Canada. More than fifty years later the threat of another similar situation was to lead to expansion. It was easier in 1912 to raid players. The owners of the new league, the Patrick brothers, simply scouted the best players available. In some cases they offered double the players' salaries. But in all cases the players got hefty raises. And they took them. They jumped. History would repeat itself in many ways.

To accommodate these new teams out West, two new rinks were built. But some of the rinks were too small to bring in enough fans to pay the salaries of these

high-priced heroes. Some of the clubs started to struggle
—a situation similar to the WHA, which started with
several arenas unable to accommodate even 10,000
fans. But the players were being paid as if 20,000 had
turned out. The Patricks vowed to stick it out, though.
Within a few years they reached an agreement on raiding with the NHA, and the established league, which by
now had taken control of the Stanley Cup, even agreed
to meet the new league's champion for the cup. (Remember the Super Bowl, when football's warring leagues
stopped fighting for one game only?)

In 1916 another strong ground swell for a union
rocked the NHA. Toronto's Cy Dennenny was suspended when he refused to play. He had asked to be
traded to Ottawa, where his family was and where he
had bought a new home. As Dennenny sat on the side-
lines he spoke to other players, warning that it could
happen to them. Players openly and angrily began talking about unions, which in those days was tantamount
to adopting communism. The other owners pleaded with
Toronto to reinstate Dennenny and trade him to Ottawa
to keep him happy. After two months, Ottawa relented.
Dennenny was traded. Another dissident mouth was
shut.

The NHA became the NHL in 1917. It was stronger
and had rid itself of its more eccentric owners. Within a
few years it buried the western league and brought its
players back within the fold. It had accomplished this by
the simple expedient of paying its players high enough
salaries. When the western loop raided the players, its
payroll soared to such heights it was unable to continue.

In 1925 another player revolt took shape. This one
involved a whole team. Hamilton had finished first and
was getting ready for the playoffs. But first, the players

wanted new contracts. They argued that when they originally had signed, the season was only twenty-four games long. Now it had been increased to a thirty-game season, but they were being paid the old rates. The president of the NHL, Frank Calder, refused to listen to the team's demands. In fact, he barred them from the playoffs and the right to compete for the Stanley Cup. He decided that the winner of the playoffs between the second-place and third-place teams would be the league's new champions.

Calder was unable to resolve the situation when the following season was ready to start. The Hamilton players still were under suspension. Calder took drastic action. He kicked Hamilton out of the National Hockey League and made all the players available. Then a franchise was awarded to the New York Americans. They were given the right to talk to all the Hamilton players, and they signed most of them. Now the players no longer were with Hamilton, and there could be no strike. Hamilton didn't exist any longer.

Although everyone in the NHL was a bona fide professional, the thought still was abhorrent to some. Making money had been something hockey players had been doing for only fifteen years. It still wasn't really nice. So when the now legendary Conn Smythe took over the Toronto Maple Leafs in 1926 he set about looking for players who were "sportsmen." Smythe was a great believer in God and country, a World War I veteran who had changed the team's original name from the "St. Patrick's" to a more patriotic-sounding nickname. The Maple Leaf, after all, was the symbol of Canada and all it stood for. Money to play the great Canadian game should always come second, believed Smythe. First, of course, was the playing, the love of the game, the competition between honest gentlemen. These were the real values. Okay, so what if Smythe drew a salary when he ran amateur clubs, and even boasted of his $1,000 bets?

His repugnance when his players talked of money even caused him to unload Babe Dye, who wound up with history's second-best goal-a-game average. "Dye," complained Smythe, "was more like a union man than a sportsman." Getting rid of Dye was one of Smythe's first acts. He refused to regret it even though Dye wound up the league's fourth-leading scorer the season he was traded.

Few of hockey's hierarchy have been able to adjust to the game's dramatic changes since, although none of them is quite in Smythe's league when it comes to outdated and vague concepts of "sportsmanship." Then again, few people around today are as successful as Smythe. Despite his views, he molded winners at Toronto.

Today, you hear more and more general managers and coaches speaking of the need to adjust to the realism of the 1970s. Some do it reluctantly, some embrace it, and others say the hell with it. Virtually every g.m. or coach in the big leagues these days is a product of a different era—although they definitely are getting younger and some of the leaders now are themselves products of expansion. They played in hockey's new era. For the most part, though, they played in a time when it was an honor to get to the NHL and you simply didn't question the way you were handled. At least, not if you weren't a superstar with some leverage.

When Wren Blair, the most modishly dressed g.m. in captivity and the first to use a hot-comb, took over the Minnesota North Stars in their first year he quickly grasped the need for new thinking. He was the coach-general manager, and he wanted to give up the coaching post. The problem was, he couldn't find anyone tuned in to the modern player. There were dozens of candidates, sure, but could they relate to the players of the 1960s—and could the players relate to them? It was becoming more difficult to motivate someone under the old, tried-and-true values. Sports was becoming increasingly criticized for the "winning is everything" attitude espoused by Vince Lombardi. The players also knew that their chances of being sent down to the minors had been greatly diminished. They knew they were needed.

"The problem today is finding a coach who can relate to the new breed of younger players," Blair conceded. "I'm having a hell of a time finding a coach who's young enough to talk to them. The old ways are finished. You can't tell a kid to play well for you just because you're the boss. This is going to be the biggest problem hockey is going to face over the next couple of years."

Little rumblings could be felt. There was the coach who complained that one of his rookies wasn't hungry enough, that the boy had been coddled. "Why, his parents even bought him a new car," complained the g.m. When the player read the criticism he told his boss, "On the ice I'm yours, but my private life is my own and I don't ever want to read anything about me that doesn't concern my playing."

When Fred Shero took over as coach of the Philadelphia Flyers, he immediately instituted a "no facial hair" rule. His explanation? "It's a form of discipline. And we must have discipline. And we must conform in order to win." Shero also said, "We have to catch planes pretty quickly after a game, and a fellow doesn't have time to dry his long hair after a game. That's a good way to catch a cold and miss a game." Finally, concluded the coach, "No group can be an individual. It's unity or else."

Yet, people were stunned the next year to see Cowboy Bill Flett sport a Buffalo Bill goatee for the Flyers. Others on the team had Prince Valiant hairdos. "I guess if it doesn't affect their play it's all right," said Shero. Then he confessed: "You've got to bend with the times. If long hair and sideburns and mustaches are a value to these kids, then I don't see anything wrong with them."

Still, it seemed incredible to some that the Rangers' Brad Park, holder of the NHL's only $200,000-a-year contract, sheepishly admitted that he was going to shave off his mustache. He had grown it while waiting for an injured leg to heal. He didn't play any games with it. "The old man doesn't like it," he said, referring to the Rangers' boss, Emile Francis.

Not everybody in hockey was a rebel in the new times. One of the finest players around, Frank Mahovlich, never was enchanted with the idea of a Players Association. When he missed two practices with Toronto, his coach, Punch Imlach, grabbed him and asked what the problem was. Mahovlich confessed that the pressures on joining the union had been too great, that he was being badgered by the players to join with them.

Before the team's next game Imlach held a meeting in the dressing room. He screamed at his players, "Not one of you is half the player Mahovlich is. If I ever catch any of my guys bugging someone by soliciting for the union—that player's gone." After the game the team spent the night in a railroad car, which clubs often did to save on hotel bills. In the morning the train was to take them to Detroit. Mahovlich wasn't aboard. At 5 A.M. he had jumped the team.

Mahovlich apparently didn't feel any need for the

union and the better life it promised its players. But not everyone had been in that fortunate a position. Some stars labored under contracts they had signed before they themselves realized how valuable they would be.

When Phil Esposito first joined the Chicago Black Hawks, for example, he signed a two-year deal. The first year he would be paid $10,500. The second year called for $12,500. "See, Phil, even if you get hurt the first game you're guaranteed $23,000 for two years," went the pitch. Put that way, it sounded like an awful lot of money. Esposito never stopped to think, though, that if he had become the world's greatest rookie he still couldn't get a raise. And even if he had a disappointing first season, how much could they cut him? So he scored twenty-three goals and added thirty-three assists for fifty-five points. Yet, he labored for $12,500 the second year. He was, by far, the most poorly paid twenty-goal man in the league at the time. That season he got twenty-seven goals—not bad for a $200-a-week player.

Most great strides in hockey have come only after pushing and threats. Shortly after World War II ended, and many players returned to the NHL, there was agitation for a pension plan. These men had been faced with other battles and the threat of losing their jobs in hockey didn't seem as terrible as it once had. They talked about a strike. Clarence Campbell became the league president in 1946, and one of his first acts was to establish a pension plan that has become the best in sports.

Even expansion came about because there was strong talk that a rival league would be formed in the early 1960s, with the United States West Coast as its base. The NHL had been the only major sports league that hadn't expanded. It had stayed with six clubs since 1942, and was the closest-knit organization in North

America. Only six teams, with about 120 players in the big time. These clubs also tied up most junior hockey in Canada. Imagine if baseball controlled all the Little League talent in the States, or if football and basketball controlled all the high schools, and the all-pervasive nature of the league's control can be seen. Yes, there were gifted players who never had the chance to make it to the big time. But everyone was fabulously successful. The six teams played to about 93 percent of capacity. The Detroit Red Wings used to like to say they performed before 110 percent of capacity. They had standing room.

For the first time a real threat was made to the league's status quo. A rival league would mean a player war, a dilution of the existing system under which hundreds of youngsters belonged to each team, and a lessening of the power of the NHL. There were other considerations, too. The league had never had much luck with network television in the States (although the Saturday night Montreal or Toronto telecasts were the highest rated shows in Canada). If a new league came along, television markets would be diluted.

One owner describes the league's thinking like this: "I guess everyone felt we had a nice little club here, and why tamper with it? Everything was going along fine. But I realized that every other sport had expanded. Television was becoming important to the economics of these other sports, since they couldn't keep raising ticket prices to keep up with growing expenses. I knew we had to expand, and we had to include television in our plans. One thing was sure: we didn't want a rival league around."

The way the league decided to expand had intriguing overtones, and demonstrated the way it thought. It not only was going to expand, but also it was going to double in size to twelve clubs. The target date was 1967—twenty-five years after the league had last redefined itself. It was going to take in the West Coast with Los Angeles and the San Francisco Bay area; it was going to St. Louis, Minneapolis-St. Paul, Philadelphia, and Pittsburgh. But it wasn't going into Canada. If you want to sell hockey on television in the States, you don't need Vancouver. But you do need the Midwest and the West Coast. By expanding, the NHL effectively killed off any chance a rival league had—at that point. Of course, it would cost money to enter the NHL. Each franchise went for $2 million—which meant each existing franchise would receive $2 million. Furthermore, the Chicago Black Hawks got even luckier. They had a white elephant of an arena in St. Louis that was past its prime and couldn't pay for itself. It was, however, the only decent hockey arena in that big city. So the Hawks convinced the league to award a franchise to St. Louis. Whoever played in the city would have to buy the building. Interestingly, the NHL gave St. Louis a franchise—before anyone had even made a bid for one. Eventually, the Hawks sold the old arena for $3 million to the St. Louis Blues.

Image was very important to the league. There was nothing wrong with the sound of Los Angeles, even though the Kings played in Inglewood. The Bay City team, however, actually was located in Oakland, and Oakland didn't sound, well, it didn't sound major league. Yet, it couldn't be called San Francisco. So the league decided the name would be the California Seals. That wouldn't offend anyone, they hoped. It did, though. It offended people in Oakland, who had enough identity problems with San Francisco being so close. In mid-season the name was changed to the Oakland Seals. Eventually, they became the California Golden Seals.

The Minnesota North Stars were in a different situation. They weren't in Minneapolis, and they weren't in St. Paul. They were in Bloomington, which lies between the cities. Although known as the twin cities, Minneapolis and St. Paul are similar only in the mind of anyone who doesn't live in Minnesota. There is an intense gut rivalry between the people who live in those cities, and to name the club either Minneapolis or St. Paul would have been tantamount to insuring that potential fans from one city would stay away. "Minnesota" was a nice compromise.

This doubling in size suddenly created more than 200 major league jobs for hockey players. This didn't mean necessarily that there were 200 big-leaguers available. A new term became necessary: the expansion player. But these players—and, in fact, everyone else— were in demand. For the first time in recent hockey history, players had a wedge.

Thus, when Glenn Hall was drafted by St. Louis from the established Black Hawks, he decided to "retire." Terry Sawchuk, another goalie, did the same. These old-timers knew they were in demand, that the first spot a team looked to was in the nets. Hall and Sawchuk probably doubled their salaries by electing to remain. Of course, they had no intentions of retiring. They used that as a ploy, and it worked. They were needed. Even Jacques Plante, who was thirty-nine years old, was wanted—and he hadn't played a game in three seasons. He "unretired" when he heard that significant money was available.

How significant was it? By 1967, when the great

expansion took place, hockey had no $100,000 players. Baseball had a flock of them. Football, caught in a war between leagues, was signing rookies for six figures. Basketball, which also had two leagues vying for talent, was filled with wealthy youngsters. But there was no competition for hockey players. The average bonus for signing a rookie was about $3,000. If he didn't sign with you, where was he going to play? The average salary in the NHL was about $14,000.

These figures started to rise with expansion. Now, you had to have the talent. You couldn't develop it any more since there were no more juniors a club could develop. A universal draft had been instituted—when any junior in Canada reached his twentieth birthday, he could be drafted by anyone. He didn't belong to a team automatically.

Meanwhile, dramatic changes were taking place among young people in North America. Hockey players didn't quite fit into the counter-culture, but they were affected by it—as was the Continent. True, they were the last pro athletes to sport long hair, sideburns, and mustaches—but they eventually wore them. Now that they were staying in school longer — because they couldn't play professionally until twenty—they were becoming better educated. For the first time a smattering of college-bred players wound up in the NHL. These players not only had degrees and long hair, they even dared to wear helmets—breaking with a time-honored tradition that had to do with machismo and stupidity. You simply didn't wear a helmet unless you were recovering from a concussion.

The need for all these players for the first time created a sort of independence on the players' part. One coach, reflecting on the good old days in 1968 (which today seems like the good old days for NHL general managers), moaned, "What does a kid care today if he doesn't make his club? He knows he can always land a job somewhere—with an Oakland or a Pittsburgh. The incentive's gone because he's not worried any more."

There had been some tentative attempts to test how binding NHL contracts were. There was what now seems a mini-revolt, but at the time was a major rebellion: the celebrated walk-outs from training camp in 1967. Many top names refused to report to camp or simply left. It was designed to test whether the contracts they had signed the previous seasons bound them to the team for the following campaign. The revolt was organized by the new head of the Players Association, Alan Eagleson. In a sense, the players won because management started to seek better ways to deal with lawyers and players' rights. But it was academic, really. If a player didn't sign with the team that owned him, he didn't play. All the holding out would amount to nothing if you weren't a needed star.

Within a year of expansion, hockey salaries leaped to about $22,000 in the East Division, while the expansion players in the West earned about $18,000. It was a big jump, percentagewise, but as one lawyer pointed out, "Twenty per cent of nothing is still nothing."

Despite these increases, salaries remained hard-fought. Some general managers still refused to meet with agents. Rookies started to make big money, as much as $30,000 or $40,000 for their first year, and bonuses got to the $15,000 range. Even though these youngsters were twenty years old, and had never seen that much money before, they were expected to negotiate for it on their own. With the complex tax laws in effect, and with a player having to guarantee his future, how could a twenty-year-old kid possibly negotiate a deal with a wily general manager? He couldn't. At least not by himself.

But all the options opened up when the WHA came along. The NHL at first laughed off the league. Campbell, informed that Cowboy Bill Flett had jumped from Philadelphia to the New York Raiders, snapped, "Cowboy who?" At first, Campbell was highly diplomatic about the new league. He said graciously, "We welcome a new league, it shows that the groundwork we laid in the NHL has produced enough interest for more people to come in. But," he added cautiously and dramatically, "if they attempt to raid our players, we will fight them from the ramparts."

Actually, there were few fights. The WHA believed that the NHL's reserve clause was invalid. The NHL blustered quite a bit about the clause and the sanctity of contracts—but the contract had never been tested in the courts and the old league really didn't know whether it indeed was valid. Privately, one owner hoped that if the clause wasn't valid "forever," at least the courts might rule that it was in effect an option clause—and the team had the player's service for at least one more year.

Some clubs didn't take chances. Before the WHA started raiding players, before the season was even over, the North Stars signed virtually every player on the team to new contracts. Orr and Esposito also signed new deals in midseason, and so did Bobby Clarke, the Philadelphia Flyers' Mr. Everything. In the back of their minds, most owners knew they wouldn't win if the WHA stepped in—at least, they wouldn't win on one-year deals. A long-term contract was something else. That was valid for the length of the contract. And even if the NHL could stop jumpers, the legal process would take so long that they would lose the players' services for the season, at least.

Even players who had long-term deals suddenly found they could renegotiate. There was the Rangers' Vic Hadfield, for example. He was under a two-year contract, but after he received a multi-year, $1 million offer to jump, he was given a new five-year deal to stay with the Rangers.

Money was all-pervasive. One superstar's agent even called up a newspaperman to plant a story that his client was upset because there was speculation the player had received "only" $120,000. "He really signed for about $150,000. But how does it look if you say he's earning so much less? He feels bad about that, it makes him look like a lesser player," said the agent.

Everyone was making money, and it seemed that everyone had an agent. People who could read box scores were calling themselves agents. There was one fellow who claimed he represented Vince Lombardi. He collared four pretty good players, negotiated four sensational deals, and then disclosed that he'd never even met Lombardi. Another agent was a former newspaperman whose previous experience with money had been making losing bets at the $50 window. His only former client had been a jockey, who lost a small fortune with bad investments recommended by the agent. This agent, though, wound up with several outstanding rookies.

When Denis Potvin, a junior player with the Ottawa 67s, was being wooed by both leagues while he was still an amateur, he decided to get himself a lawyer. He got two—one for the negotiations, one for the investment.

"It's complicated when your client is nineteen years

old and you're trying to provide for him when he's going to be forty-five," explained one of the lawyers.

One general manager claimed he was offered a bribe of a $3,000 television commercial if he would sign one of his prizes for what the agent was asking. The agent dismissed the charge as "ridiculous—I offered it to him because I could get 15 percent."

It was easy enough to see why players needed negotiators. One rookie was reading his contract and asked his attorney what a certain word meant. The word was "negotiate."

Some of the more unscrupulous agents had absurd schemes. One called up Esposito and offered to bargain for him, in return taking only 10 percent of whatever raise Esposito received. It was during Esposito's 126-point year, the final one under the old contract.

"Did he think I wasn't going to get a raise after getting 126 points?" Esposito wondered.

Some agents charge stiff fees—15 percent of the salary, and some of them justify it by saying that they'll get players outside endorsements, too. But one team had a pair of goalies who gave 15 percent to an agent—and never got an outside job.

At least one general manager didn't want his boss to realize how much money he was paying his players. Charlie Finley, the Seals' owner, charged that his g.m., Garry Young, "signed some players for double" the amounts he had told Finley they were receiving. This exhausted the budget.

Young later explained that, "The players would have been lost if I didn't do that." As it was, the Seals lost eleven players to the WHA. They were the hardest hit club in the NHL. Still, the players that remained, claimed Finley, "will cost me an extra $1 million. I've practically been driven out of the hockey business."

In all, about seventy players jumped. Only two, Hull and McKenzie, came from the top twenty-five scorers. Yet, it is likely that those 70 jumpers earned more than the entire NHL payroll had the season before.

At the height of the jumping, while NHL officials were bemoaning the loss of "loyalty" and the grand old traditions, the National Hockey League itself jumped— from CBS to NBC. Its contract with CBS was coming to an end. It had been receiving about $1 million a year— which was divided among the United States clubs—and had one meeting with CBS to negotiate a new deal. Everyone at CBS figured the league would come back. After all, you don't just listen to one offer and suddenly leave. You do give the man who's been paying you for a number of years a chance to raise your salary. But the league instead jumped to NBC—which offered twice as much. "I thought the NHL would at least have had the courtesy to come back and hear our second offer," moaned a CBS official. It was a statement NHL owners had made repeatedly about their own players who had jumped to the WHA.

Six

IT WAS Father's Day. Derek had returned to Niagara Falls at his father's request. There was a golf tournament for members of the company's credit union and his father had told him, "I think I can swing the credit union manager into giving me a loan for a new car. If you show up at the tournament, it'll really impress him."

"I walked into my home town. Old shirt, dirty blue jeans, three or four days' growth of beard. I go into a dealer and ask a guy for the best station wagon he's got. The guy says 'over there.' He doesn't take much interest in a young kid looking at a wagon. He figures it's not a sale. I asked him, 'You always sell cars like that, pal?' and he says, 'Well, it's got four tires and four doors.' I asked him how much and he said, '$6,700.' And I said, 'How much is your commission on $6,700?' and he said, 'It's enough.' I told him, 'Not on this one it's not.' "

Derek went to another dealer, got a wagon, and had the owner put dealer plates on it. Then he drove it home.

His father was sleeping upstairs. "Come on down, Dad, I want to show you something," said Derek. Harold Sanderson put on a bathrobe and walked outside. When he saw the car he ran upstairs, and began pacing. "What are you doing, Dad?" asked Derek. "I got to think about this," replied Harold. "I never dreamed of anything like this." And then he started to cry and hugged Derek. Then he woke Caroline and she started to cry.

Derek was thinking: "It's only a car. Only money."

"It wasn't happening to me. I was acting out a dream," says Derek. "I had been thinking about going to Philadelphia for so long and so hard, that I was flooded. I was numb."

But numb enough to be able to suggest to the Blazers that when they brought him in for the formal signing Harold should be on hand. A dual signing. All in the family.

Derek "pasted a smile" on his face at nine in the morning and wore it until five at night. The contract, of course, was already signed but a big show was made in Kennedy Plaza in Philadelphia. About 5,000 people showed up and Derek spoke of the new attitude that would come to this city of losers, where all the athletic teams were happy to play .500. There were posters of Derek and McKenzie and Parent. "The town is filled with losers," Derek told the waiting world. "It's been conditioned to lose so much that the players were losers the minute they set foot in the city."

Then he was whisked away in a police car. On the drive back to the signing party at a hotel, Derek and the policeman spoke and Derek told him how much he admired the mayor, Frank Rizzo, who had been elected on a law-and-order platform. "It seems sort of funny, me being a law-and-order guy," Derek concedes. Derek wanted to know where the power was in Philadelphia, who made things run, what the people thought of Rizzo. He was attracted to Rizzo. He told the policeman that he intended to work with the Police Athletic League. He was going to get his chance to work with poor youngsters.

But first, there was the party. Cooper's children were there, and Derek played with them and posed with them. But he got annoyed when a woman, whom he didn't know, insisted that he pose for pictures, too. He found out it was Bernie Brown's daughter, and Bernie Brown happened to be the man who put up most of the money for the Philadelphia Blazers. In effect, he was Derek's boss.

"Funny that I'd never met Brown before," says Derek. "Here he goes and commits himself for over two and a half million and he never even met me. Right away I didn't like the scene. The way his daughter was acting, I felt as if he'd bought a toy for his kids. I didn't get good vibes. But I was hoping that maybe I wouldn't have to see that much of him."

Sanderson, though, committed himself to making it in his new surroundings, although he still was saddled by a combination of nervousness and nostalgia. "I was going to come to town with a cocky conservatism," he explains. "No more being brash. I was going to reject the swinger, the rookie, image. I wanted to be known as a more settled individual. I just wanted a nice quiet relationship with a couple of friends. I'd even met Jack Kelly, you know, Grace's brother, real Philadelphia class. That was it. There was going to be class surrounding me and the things I did. Clean up the act. Take out the Esquire shoe polish."

The summer flew by. He couldn't focus on the

Philadelphia Blazers. It was all too unreal—the money, the parties, the signing, the fame, the interviews. But all of it was for one end—he was supposed to play. And not for Boston any more. For a new team in a new league. In the past he knew where he was going when he was to report to training camp. There'd be people he knew, an identity he was familiar with. Now it was a new ball game, with new players. Oh, maybe the rules were the same. But it really was time to play now. How much of what had happened the previous weeks had really happened to Derek Sanderson, Philadelphia Blazer, and not Derek Sanderson, Boston Bruin?

"I was a day late for camp. It was wrong. I knew it. And it started as a disaster. It was just that I was in a bad frame of mind. The money was new and I was spending it pretty good. But I hadn't had to work for it yet. And I'm not sure I came prepared to work for it. I was catered to, primped, and pampered. And hell, I liked it."

Strange, that when he arrived in Toronto to get a connecting flight to Ottawa for his first exhibition game no one made a fuss over him. But not far away Derek could see the glaring headlights of hundreds of cars stalled in a traffic jam, and he could hear people shouting and bands playing and children screaming. They weren't there for Derek Sanderson, though. They were welcoming home the triumphant National Hockey League players on Team Canada, after their truth-is-stranger-than-fiction victory over the Russians.

"I stood in the crowd and watched as the players were getting off the plane. No one recognized me. And I watched these guys getting off, after one of the greatest hockey series ever played, when a whole country pulled together like it never had before, and these guys were heroes, and I said to myself: 'I could have been there.' I had been invited by Sinden, but then they cut me after I jumped. I could have been part of this. Damn it, the money isn't worth it. I should have taken the hundred thousand a year from the Bruins. But I had to be greedy, and there I was, going for an exhibition game against the Ottawa Nationals while my teammates, my countrymen, were coming home from Russia."

Derek took his connecting flight, though, "and second by second as we got closer I was regretting it. I felt my past getting further and further away, an important part of me was in that airport in Toronto and that was where I knew I belonged."

Because of the hassle at the airport, Derek didn't get to the game on time. He still hadn't met many of the players, especially those who had been rescued from the $200-a-week obscurity of the Eastern League. Because his Bruins' contract ran until September 30, he hadn't been able to work out with the Blazers—who were to open the season in less than two weeks. Although he missed camp, and despite the fact that he hardly knew most of the men, McKenzie had appointed Derek the team captain. The captain headed for the hotel, and had a few beers as he waited for the game to end and his new teammates to arrive.

"The first time I saw the guys I was stunned. No shirts, no ties, nothing. Blue jeans. I said to McKenzie that he's got to get a dress rule on the club. Okay, maybe the guys didn't know how to dress, but we were going to show them."

It struck Sanderson immediately that "the attitude of the guys toward me wasn't the friendliest in the world." He was worried. He guessed it was because of the money. McKenzie acted as he always did, and Parent, the first big jumper, didn't appear concerned. But ironically, Plumb was bothered by Sanderson's money. Yet, if it hadn't been for Sanderson—and Cooper attempting to show Woolf that he was serious—Plumb wouldn't have received a 600 percent raise to jump to the Blazers.

"On that first bus ride with the guys we went back to our training camp in Sherbrooke. I just had a bad taste in my mouth the whole trip. I just had the feeling that it wasn't going to work out. I sat in the back by myself."

Still, Derek claims he tried, working himself into shape. No one came out and mentioned the money directly to him. But Derek was doing all the buying and one night, over some beers, the money thing came out.

"I realize now I shouldn't have been buying," says Derek. "That was definitely wrong. I was trying to buy their respect and you can't do that. I was the captain, the guy they were supposed to look up to, and I thought this was the way you went around doing that. Later, Bobby Orr told me that you just don't go around buying and picking up tabs. Sure, Bobby said, some guys might think you're a cheap son of a bitch, especially since you're making ten times more than the next guy. But in the long run you're respected more because you haven't bought anyone."

That was all forgotten as Sanderson was about to wear the day-glo orange and yellow Blazer uniform for the first time in game conditions. It was in Quebec City against the Nordiques. For the first time he and the other stars, McKenzie and Parent, were on the ice together and it started off beautifully. The first minute of play the Nordiques got a penalty and the Blazers would have a power play.

This was what Sanderson had waited for all those

years with the Bruins—he would be the pivot, the center, when his club had a man advantage. Esposito wouldn't be out there the whole two minutes. He wouldn't, in fact, be out there at all. Derek was starting on the power play, those golden chances when a good scorer can increase his season's goal total by 30 percent. Derek was at center. McKenzie was his right wing, Bryan Campbell his left wing. Plumb was at the right point and Andre Lacroix on the left.

"I won the face-off," Derek recalls. "I gave it to Lacroix, who gave it to Plumb. I was circling, then I broke free between two guys and I had the puck. There was McKenzie breaking down the right side. I dumped it through. But Johnny turned for the puck, lost his balance, hit the goal post. He broke his arm. And that was the dream gone—all the superstar money they had put up, we didn't play together except for that first thirty seconds."

It got worse, according to Sanderson. McKenzie had his broken arm, and then was involved in the big court case that was to eventually permit all the jumpers to remain in the WHA. Parent, nervous, excitable, one day left his net in the middle of a practice, skated off the ice, went into the dressing room, and took off his gear.

"I quit," he told Sanderson. "I just don't like this whole set-up. I don't want to play here."

Sanderson, who found himself in charge by default, told Parent, "We've got to stick it out. A lot of people's lives are hinging on us—guys in this league, guys in the NHL. They're all trying for wedges in their contracts and none of it will mean shit unless we make this league go."

It is probable Sanderson only halfheartedly believed those words. Parent did—for the moment. The next day he walked off again, and again Sanderson scampered after him and brought him back.

With McKenzie temporarily gone, with Parent finding himself unhappy, with Sanderson torn in a sense between two worlds, a stabilizer was needed. "Then Phil Watson came on the scene," says Derek. "He put in with Brown, not Cooper. It got discouraging for me. One time Watson didn't like what we were doing and he jumped over the boards and came onto the ice, pitter-patting in his sneakers and he starts to show us the various positions—like we're all junior B's."

Derek, though, was looking forward to his first exhibition game at Sherbrooke. This was, after all, his new training-camp home. The people, he thought, would be delighted. They had a major-league team training in their own home town. Fifty-six people showed up for the game.

"Pride went out the window right there. God, was it discouraging—to say the least. There was no one to show off to, no one to perform in front of, no ego booster, incentive, drive. The ego of the professional athlete is so supreme that even money at times can't compensate for it. It's uppermost in the athletes' mind at all times. The only guy I ever met who doesn't have an ego is Dallas Smith. With Dallas, it was strictly money. You hear guys say that money's the only thing. Hell, I haven't met a guy yet who enjoyed being benched even though he's receiving his money. Donnie Awrey always used to say he didn't care. But in the '73 playoffs he had a meeting with Sinden over being benched. I didn't like to be insulted when those fifty-six people showed up. Yet, I imagined how the owners felt, trying to pay expenses with fifty-six people in the stands. Still, I thought I'd stick it out. I chalked this up to the fact that the people in Sherbrooke just didn't know better, that they didn't believe we were a reality."

When Sanderson would see old friends again— Cheevers, or Wayne (Swoop) Carleton of Ottawa—he'd notice they were laughing on the ice, "as if this was some big joke. But I think they were laughing at the money they were getting. I know Cheevers was intense to get this thing off the ground. He's a winner, and if the club didn't win, he'd take it personally."

Meanwhile, Sanderson continued to try to buy his teammates. He'd drop $100 for dinner with half a dozen players, he'd lend someone $150 if they asked for $50. And he was attempting to reconcile the various factions. There was, he explains, "the French group, the guys from the National League, the guys from the Eastern League, and some guys who just wanted to do a whole different number."

McKenzie, he says, "was the only one who let me keep my sanity. Just having him around seemed to make it all right. I'd been with him at Boston from the beginning. I talked to him about this whole scene and he admitted that it bothered him, too, and that he was sorry he was out of the National League. Soon, I got the feeling that he was past caring. His ideas were stepped on by Watson, who had really worked his way in. Watson was supposed to be a scout for us but he worked his way up and Brown was listening to him.

"And I started to realize that my ego was too big for this. Maybe if I was a different sort of person it would have been important for me to try to build this. But I had to have it right then. I had to have 20,000 people at

Madison Square Garden hating me. I'd rather have 20,000 people who hate me and throw stuff at me than fifty-six people who love me."

The first World Hockey Association game that Derek Sanderson played in was at Boston, inevitably. It was, in fact, the first game for the Blazers and the New England Whalers. His old teammate, Ted Green, now was the captain of the Whalers, a club headed by Jack Kelley and containing many players from New England. The prospect of a Green-Sanderson confrontation attracted the largest crowd the WHA would boast of its first campaign—14,442.

Derek scored the WHA's first goal at Boston. "I can remember that, just like I can remember the pass that sent McKenzie to the hospital," says Derek. "Before the game me and Teddy had a phony face-off, you know for the photographers. The ovation was something. Greenie was laughing and we shook hands. I asked him what he thought and he said, 'Well, it's a go. It's for real.' "

"The game was a few minutes old when Don O'Donoghue set me up. I went in on Al Smith, got it over him, jammed the puck under the crossbar. And it was the first goal. Sanderson, from O'Donoghue and Jim Cardiff at 6:52."

The crowd went wild. It stood and screeched for Derek who smiled genuinely. It wasn't a smirk. It was a gut reaction. That didn't last long, though. "At the end of the first period I'd shot my wad. I had nothing left. I was on the ice for the losing goal when I missed my man. I was too tired to even reach for him and he walked around me with about three minutes left and shot it into the net."

The Whalers won, 4-3. But at the end of the game

Sanderson and Green had tied for the first star. "We shook hands. Here we were, two ex-Boston Bruins trying to start a whole new league."

There was, strangely, no elation on Derek's part when it was over. Instead, it was simply the feeling of a loss. A game was over that he hadn't won. There was no heightened sense of the historic, no jubilation that at last the league had got off the ground and Derek Sanderson had scored the first goal back in his old town. Indeed, the aftermath of that game he remembers most vividly. Cooper and Brown flew in all their friends, and on the flight back to Philadelphia he had to sign autographs for his owners' neighbors.

Perhaps it would change the next night—opening night in Philadelphia against the same Whalers.

The inside of the Philadelphia Civic Center brings back visions of a grand old movie house—perhaps the Roxy of New York. It has the feel of the 1930s—French panels on the ceiling. One looks for the giant organ. And then, incredibly, at one end of the ice there is a stage. It is a huge stage with raised curtains and a spectator couldn't be blamed for imagining that the lights will dim and a screen will drop and *Gone with the Wind* will be reeled off.

At ice level there are orchestra seats only eight rows deep. The remaining seats, colored orange and red, slope up steeply like an arena. It is the only part of the building that presents an arena-like appearance.

Derek left his $26-a-day room at the Holiday Inn for his first look at the building. He arrived about 11:30 A.M. for the team meeting and the light skate that usually precedes a night game. His first impression of the rink was, he says, "a downer." The boards were made of fiberglass and the pipes supporting the boards were an eyesore. The rink was smaller than regulation width in order to allow people in the side balcony to see the ice. If it hadn't been cut down, the fans wouldn't have been able to see the floor since their line of sight ended about ten feet from the edge of the boards. The ice was bad, but Derek figured it could be fixed by game time.

When he arrived for the game the guard wouldn't let him into the parking lot. Derek had forgotten to ask for a parking pass. "But I'm a player," he told the guard. "Where's your pass?" he was asked. Derek Sanderson, world's highest paid player, then took his Continental Mark IV and parked it in a lot across the street.

He had no trouble getting into the building, though. He looked at the rink and then went up two flights of stairs to the locker room. Most rinks have the players' room adjacent to the rink. Here there was a pretty good walk—on skates, of course—up two flights. If someone had to go to the trainer's room, there was still another flight to maneuver.

There was a sign over the whirlpool that warned malingerers: "You're no good to the club in the tub or in the pub." Omens. The sweaters were too tight. Sanderson wasn't that crazy about the uniform to start with. He insists they were designed in the color scheme of Mrs. Cooper's bathroom "because she happened to like those colors." Another thing about those bright orange and yellow colors: "They gave out a glare and you couldn't see anything. Absolutely the ugliest colors you ever saw in your life." Then there was the stick problem. "A lot of the guys' sticks just didn't arrive. I guess the big companies didn't want to send in a couple of hundred sticks until they were paid. They didn't want to get stuck in case the league folded. The ones that did come in—some of them weren't even the right sticks." Bryan Campbell's sticks were for a right-handed shooter. He shoots left.

A pretty good-sized crowd of about 7,500 was on hand. "So we go out for our warmups, and the guys are falling down—not one or two guys, but seven or eight. No one even wanted to skate in circles. I looked around the rink and I couldn't believe it. The place looked like a curling rink it was so small. There was a two-inch space between the ice and the boards, just a hole." That's where they had rearranged the rink dimensions so the fans could see. When the rink had been chopped up to diminish its size, the pipes through which the coolant brine flowed weren't embedded in concrete. They had been buried in sand and covered with sawdust. Water, however, drains right through sawdust that isn't tightly packed. Thus, a thin surface of ice (known as shell ice) had formed, but there was water underneath it.

This shell ice supported the players. Unfortunately, the Zamboni ice-cleaning machine had never been used on the surface. It didn't arrive until just before game-time. While the players warmed up, mechanics were feverishly assembling the huge tank-like vehicle. When it finally took the ice, it went right through. Chunks were dug over the ice, but the show had to go on. Derek was called to center ice to face off against Green. Mayor Rizzo came out for the ceremonial puck-dropping.

"What a mess this is," said Rizzo to Sanderson.

"You don't want to be a part of this fiasco, do you?" Sanderson asked, then suggested, "Why don't you just drop the puck and get the hell out of here?"

"You know, Derek," said the mayor, "You're the only one with any brains around here. I'm leaving."

He dropped the puck and left Green and Sanderson.

Derek turned to Green and said, "Someone's going to get killed." Green replied, "You're right, but who ever heard of a hockey game called off because of holes in the ice?"

Referee Bill Friday—another jumper from the NHL —then made his first call in the new league. He called off the game. That immediately angered the Blazers' fans. Each of them was armed with an orange puck, given as a souvenir of the momentous occasion. They began hurling the pucks at Friday, his linesmen, Cooper, the score clock. More orange pucks wound up on the ice than would ever see WHA duty. The pucks, it seemed, took funny bounces. All pucks are frozen before a game to give them truer bounces. But the orange pucks simply refused to freeze and they were taken out of circulation. They made pretty good missiles, though.

While the fans were complaining, the players were having their own argument, not aware the game had been canceled. They were arguing over who should be the first one onto the ice—no one wanted the honor. "There's a tradition with most clubs in the way you go out," explains Derek. "In Boston it was very rigid. Each guy had his own order. But here, there was no tradition and no one wanted it. I think we were all afraid of what might happen to the first guy on the ice."

It became academic after the game was called. Derek was ready to take the ice when he was told there was no contest. "Well, I was the captain so I had to tell the guys. Then I got undressed. I heard the fans were acting up, so I put my uniform back on and went out to calm them down. Hell, I didn't blame them for being angry. They had to shell out $8.50 for a top seat. The Flyers of the NHL were only charging $7.50. Then the fans couldn't find parking spaces, everything about going to the place was a hassle, and then it turned out they couldn't even see a game. I apologized on behalf of the club and told them not to run over each other in the parking lot."

Somehow, things got worse. In fact, when Derek played his first game as a Blazer at Madison Square Garden "it became the most humiliating defeat of my life."

This was his second game in the new league, and it brought him down to earth—perhaps more so than his experience in the Philadelphia fiasco had. The Garden was, of course, the world's most famous arena. It was here that he had performed regularly before capacity crowds of 17,250. The last time he had appeared there— five months before—the place had been packed and the Bruins had won the Stanley Cup. He hadn't been in the Garden since. Now he was wearing that strange uniform, with the L in Blazer shaped like a hockey stick. He was a diamond plucked from Tiffany's window and put in Klein's basement. The crowd was announced as 5,132 people. It was as if he were appearing in a huge, sparsely inhabited living room. More than 12,000 empty pastel-colored seats stared down at him as he took the ice. The boos echoed hollowly in the vast deserted cavern. But they were booing disjointedly, not the roaring hatred that he had become accustomed to and, yes, loved. It was quite perfunctory, as if the fans were giving an imitation of what their more high-born cousins, the Ranger fans, were accustomed to doing. It was a kids' crowd, leather jackets, sloppy hair, lower middle class. And there were even a few dozen blacks—that rarest of all ethnic groups at hockey games—because of the presence of the only black in major-league hockey, the Raiders' Alton White. "Geez," said one of the Blazers before the game, "speaking about insults, how'd you like to be traded for Alton White?"

One felt embarrassed for Sanderson, skating at half-speed, often in the right place but tapping his stick in vain on the ice as his teammates failed to heed his signals. They didn't give him the puck. Sometimes he skated behind the net and held the puck there for lingering moments—longer than anyone normally would dare —and the inexpert Raider defense, which included the tubby Kent Douglas who had played the night before for the Long Island Ducks of the Eastern League, couldn't touch him. But Sanderson had no one to pass the puck to.

Soon, the crowd stopped booing when he had the puck. It was obvious neither he nor his Halloween-clothed teammates could do them any damage. By the end of the game he was weak and discouraged. The Blazers were shut out, 5-0, and the man who turned in the blanking—described by WHA publicists as the league's first shutout "east of Cleveland"—was someone named Pete Donnelly. Donnelly had been an engineering student in the Midwest the year before. When he heard about the WHA he found a way to make some quick money. This was his first major league game.

As Sanderson left the ice at game's end he noticed the Rangers' Hadfield watching and Hadfield laughed and asked him how the Philadelphia Zamboni was doing.

The Raiders' Jamie Kennedy headed for the New York dressing room and shook his head. "I don't believe it," said Kennedy. "I went out there in the first period and I pinned Sanderson against the boards and I thought I'd get an elbow. But he said, 'Thanks, I was getting tired.' "

In the Philadelphia dressing room Sanderson was

disgusted. The embarrassment showed and many reporters were to say later that they felt sorry for him. Perhaps this league would indeed succeed one day, but this was hardly a major league beginning.

"I'm fed up with myself," said Sanderson. "I regret taking the money. I really should give back half of it. I think I'm overpaid."

The next day he bought himself a Rolls-Royce.

"It was a rainy day and I had nothing else to do," Derek explains. "I was wearing blue jeans and a sweat shirt, and I walked in and saw something I liked." According to Derek, the conversation went like this:

"What's that over there?"

"A Silver Shadow with a long wheelbase."

"Okay, that's the one I want."

"Are you kidding? That's $31,000."

Later, reflecting on the price of the car, and other things that were to become part of his life, Derek said, "The money took away insecurity. Becoming a millionaire gave me a confidence I had never known. Take flying. It stopped bothering me. I realized I could have whatever I wanted, do whatever I wanted. And things suddenly stopped becoming a hassle. If I wanted to spend 400 bucks on a woman, take her out and buy her something, I could do it. If I wanted to run away to Vegas for a few days, I could do that, too. Money gave me options."

Derek now had his car, his money, his captaincy. The latter was the first to go. "I knew the players were resenting me and the money," he says. "After the Ranger game I told McKenzie the best thing for everybody was for the players to vote whether they wanted a captain. I guess it was sort of like a vote of confidence. If they wanted a captain, I'd remain. If not, I was out. Four players voted to keep me. The rest? Ten said no and four abstained."

The Blazers finally opened—after their second scheduled game also was called off—against the Cleveland Crusaders and Sanderson's old friend, Cheevers, who next to Orr had been the Bruin most respected by his teammates. Cheevers, a horseplayer who read "The Racing Form" before games, hoped that one day he would write a first-person book told by a horse on the eve of the Kentucky Derby.

Sanderson didn't get much chance to do any damage to Cheevers, or to show off in front of his new fans. His left shoulder was separated by Skip Krake. "I played for appearance's sake," relates Derek. "They popped the shoulder in and I went back. Sure, I played with the pain. But hockey players are accustomed to skating with pain. As a rule, we don't pop pills. No kidding. I hear that football players pop bennies and greenies, but we don't. Anyway, I played with the shoulder like that and it was going to take me some time to recuperate." That same game the Blazers had an even more severe injury—Parent stuck out his foot to knock away a shot by Krake and broke a bone. Thus, within a few weeks the Blazers had lost the effectiveness of their three prize jumpers—Sanderson, McKenzie, and Parent.

The Rolls was quite a job. It had a divider ("the only model in the United States with a divider," says the owner) and it had a beautiful burgundy exterior. The inside, swathed in leather, was soft and woody. Derek drove the car himself when he went looking for his mansion. At first, Woolf was apoplectic at the thought of a $31,000 investment. Then he figured, "What the heck, it's good for Derek. He's got an image to uphold, and anyway a Rolls is as good an investment as there is. You can always get most of your money back, especially if you're Derek Sanderson. The car's worth more just because he drives it." Derek could afford the $85 Rolls charged for a washing. After all, every two weeks he received a check for $25,000—with, of course, $12,000 deducted for income tax.

The house that grabbed Sanderson's eye was priced at $150,000. It had 14 rooms on a few acres. "I'm going to get a chauffeur and a valet," Derek said in a proclamation. Woolf went along, again for the same reasons he permitted the luxury of the Rolls. But when it came time to sign a contract, the seller backed out. Undaunted, Derek looked again. This time he looked in Merion, the posh Philadelphia suburb. This house had 14 bedrooms, with an 80-foot ballroom. He took a drive out there one day.

The house should have been used for *Last Year in Marienbad*. It had fourteen fountains, "all working," said Derek proudly as he explained that the house and grounds "belonged to the Edgar Allan Poe estate." The driveway, which culminated in a circle with a diameter of fifty feet, was paved with different color bricks. There was a servants' quarters and a livery stable. The bath house overlooked a seventy-five-foot-long pool that stood next to an elephant-shaped fountain. On one side of the house, going back 100 feet, was a fifty-foot-wide stretch of grass that could have been used for cricket or softball or touch football. At the end of the field was the white marble gazebo. Beyond that were five acres of rolling country. The mansion on the next estate in the distance, past the clay tennis courts, was an eyesore compared to his.

Derek by now was ensconced at the Latham, a low-keyed Philadelphia hotel, where he lived in a $125-a-day suite. The lifestyle was becoming a regular routine, although it is doubtful any athlete anywhere in the world at the age of twenty-six was living quite this way. Still, it started to come around for Derek. As each game passed, his shoulder strengthened and he felt himself getting into shape. Each shift he was able to last a little longer. Unfortunately for him and the Blazers, though, they couldn't win a game. A healthy Parent might have given them the quick start so important to a new season, when the goalies are ahead of the shooters. But Parent's replacements were Marcel Paille, who at the age of forty was playing for his tenth professional team, and Yves Archambault, who was known to few people.

On November 1, Derek Sanderson played his last game for the World Hockey Association. And it was his best one. The opponent was Cleveland, against his friendly nemesis, Cheevers. As Derek was leaving the ice in the third period someone in the pro-Cleveland crowd threw a piece of paper on the ice. (Someone later suggested it was a $100 bill that had fallen out of Derek's wallet.) Derek didn't see the paper, but he turned to move out of the way of a linesman. As he twisted, he caught the paper with his skate and wrenched his back. He suffered a herniated disc. The pain, worse, much worse, than a funnybone being jabbed, shot through his back and legs as vertebra hit nerve.

"I tried to come back. They taped it up for me, but I didn't realize how bad it was. I went out on the ice again and then I had to leave. God, it was awful. That night I slept with a plastic bag filled with ice, keeping it on my back. I thought that would help. But in the morning it was worse than ever."

Derek was placed in a wheelchair and flown back to Philadelphia, where his hospital stay began. It was the

Sanderson, Attorney Bob Woolf and Blazer Owner Jim Cooper at signing of 2.6 million dollar contract.

Top: Sanderson serving at Bachelors III. *Bottom:* Former Boston teammate and later player-coach of the Blazers, John McKenzie welcomes Sanderson to Philadelphia. *Opposite:* "The Turk" discussing hockey strategy.

Sanderson pondering a reporter's question. *Opposite:* Joe Namath and Derek Sanderson meeting the press.

Al Ruelle

UPI

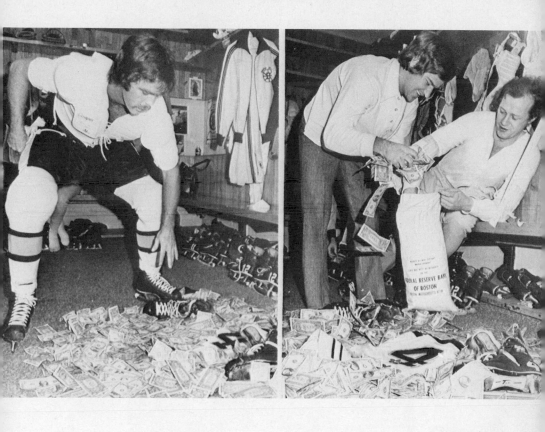

Sanderson and Bobby Orr working out payment of a bet as to who would marry first. Derek lost (Orr married first) and dumped $1,000 in dollar bills and pennies on the floor of the Bruin's dressing room. *At right,* Orr, with teammate Wayne Cashman helping, makes the collection. *Opposite, top:* A relaxed Sanderson watches the Bruins practice. *Bottom:* Sanderson and young admirer after returning to the Boston Bruins.

Opposite: The captain of the Philadelphia Blazers leaves the ice after the opening home game was cancelled because officials found the ice surface unfit to play on. *Above:* Sanderson's Rolls Royce: $31,000 to buy and $85 to wash.

The pad in Boston.

More of the pad. Derek's portrait, done in pastels, hangs at right.

Sanderson keeps Bobby Hull away from the puck. *Opposite, top:* Derek and Vic Hadfield of the Rangers. The two tangled in the 1973 Stanley Cup Playoffs. *Bottom:* Sanderson on the move against the New York Rangers.

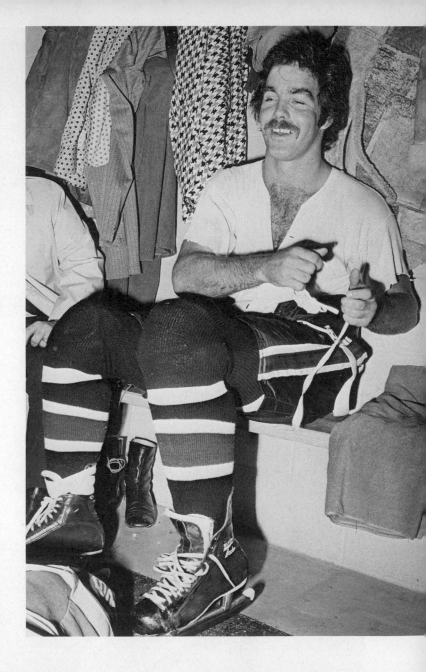

Keeping the press happy. *Opposite, top:* The puck is somewhere under Sanderson. *Bottom:* "Should I go over the boards and join the fight?"

Sanderson and his attorney, Bob Woolf, on the patio of his pent-house apartment in Boston.

beginning of the end. He had performed in eight games and had scored three goals and three assists.

The sign on the door said "No Visitors." But orthopedic men and gastrointestinal specialists walked in and out continually. The fabulous invalid was the object of curiosity. He was in an awful state. The G.I. specialist checked on his colitis, which had flared up again. The orthopedic man attempted to heal his back.

Nurses flitted in and out. Derek looked weary when a girl, about twenty, who he'd never seen before, disregarded the sign and walked in and asked for his autograph. She left and he was alone with a visitor. "Pour me some of that," he said, and pointed to a half-filled bottle of Canadian Club. "With a little water." He then unwrapped the ham-and-cheese hero his visitor had brought him, took a bite, and washed it down with the C.C. and water. Then he grubbed a cigarette.

The telephone rang. It was a woman checking his credit references for the house he wanted to buy.

"How old?" Derek asked. "I'm twenty-six."

Another question followed. Derek answered: "How much this year? Oh, $400,000."

The caller obviously was satisfied.

"Now that I've got the Rolls," he said, "I've got it all planned. I can't take any more of this pressure. Too much, too many people. I've got to get away. I'll have my valet and my chauffeur. When it's time to go to a game I'll get into my car, and sit down in the back and I'll pick up a newspaper and read it. And that's how I'll be a hockey player. I've had enough of four walls in my life."

He was interrupted by a student nurse who walked in holding two needles. "What gauge are they?" he asked nervously. Could it be that Derek Sanderson is concerned about the width of two needles? "I don't know the gauge," she answered, "but one's blue and one's green." He took the green needle, satisfied that it wasn't too thick. "I'm going to bleed," he said, "all over these $75 silk pajamas." He then explained to the nurse the proper way to inject the needle into his buttocks so that it would give him a minimum of pain.

"Go home and practice on a sausage," he told her.

Soon, one of his doctors told him about an attractive student nurse. "Hi," Derek said on the intercom. "I hear there's a pretty student nurse on the floor. Would you send her in with some ginger ale?" "I'll see what I can do," came the reply. Within five minutes the nurse had made three appearances in his private room, and had accepted an invitation to be among the 200 guests at his housewarming.

During his three weeks in the hospital he began to bad-mouth the Blazers. "I guess Derek was upset," says the paternal Cooper. "And he said a lot of things in the hospital that didn't help the situation. Things weren't going so well anyway, but Derek kept criticizing and I guess that helped keep the fans away."

By now, Watson had replaced McKenzie as the coach. McKenzie was getting ready to return soon, and with Parent almost available perhaps things would look up. But Parent did a strange thing while he was waiting for his foot to heal. He had a circumcision. A doctor had told him, "Since you're waiting to return, why don't you have it done?" When Cooper found out about it, he couldn't believe it. In any event, the circumcision took longer to heal than the foot, and Parent missed more games even though his broken foot bone had healed. But he couldn't wear a jock strap.

For a week after Derek left the hospital he loafed around. He got on skates finally and said he would be ready to return in another few days. Maybe things would work out after all. By Christmas the three heroes—Sanderson, McKenzie, and Parent—would have their various extremities in working order and then things would be different.

Harold Sanderson, meanwhile, finally had a player he was ready to deliver. The club's $25,000-a-year scout told Watson about Tom Cottringer, a 215-pound part-time, semipro goalie from Niagara Falls who had just lost his job with the Welland Chemical Company. Watson was dubious (Sanderson secretly believed that Watson, a French-Canadian, wanted only French-Canadian goalies). Anyway, Watson didn't want to give Cottringer a once-over. Derek then offered to pay Cottringer's expenses to Philadelphia. This, Watson accepted.

Cottringer was about 30 pounds overweight when he reported to the Cherry Hill Arena in New Jersey for a workout. Watson couldn't tell much and was leery of trying him under game conditions. As luck would have it, though, the Greensboro Generals of the Eastern League were to play in Cherry Hill that night and didn't have a healthy goalie. The Greensboro coach asked Watson if one was available. Watson was delighted to lend him Cottringer. Now he could see how he would do under game conditions. Cottringer turned in a shutout.

Now he waited for his chance. A few games went by and the Blazers' goalies, Paille and Archambault, got bombed. The time was ripe for Cottringer to make his debut. He won his first start, an overtime game, and he became a minor celebrity. The next game he started again and went into the final period leading by 3-1. But the Blazers lost in overtime, 4-3, and Cottringer was sent back home. Oddly, his 1-1 record was the best of the five goalies that had been used by the Blazers. But with his departure, Harold Sanderson's last "find" was gone from the scene.

Whenever Derek picked up a paper or looked at the television set, it seemed to him he was being rapped. "He's getting $2,300 a day and he's defrauding the public, they'd say. They would complain that I hadn't done a thing yet. That I was a crybaby and a thief."

Woolf remembers the day that Derek had been admitted to the hospital. "I was in Philadelphia to look at the house we were thinking of getting. Then I heard he was coming back from Cleveland. I got to the hospital and saw him being wheeled in. He looked awful. Then he said to me, 'How do you like this? Just when I'm getting it all together. For the first time, I really felt good.' The night before he had a goal and two assists. That goal against Cheevers, why, he said it was the biggest thrill of his life. But now, at the time he really could have begun to make it big, he was laid up."

After Derek was released from the hospital, he started to feel he wasn't wanted any more. On December 1 he put on the skates again and started to work out. He told the club he thought he would be ready in a week, when the Raiders would be coming to Philadelphia. By this time, most people who were associated with the club now agree, Bernie Brown had decided he had to get rid of Derek.

"You know, I think the first thing Brown did in the morning, before taking his glass of orange juice, was to read the contract and try to figure how he could lose me," says Derek.

Cooper and Brown had already been arguing vehemently. Money was getting tight. McKenzie, Parent, Sanderson, the bad ice, a losing team—all conspired to keep away the fans.

Recalls Cooper: "That last game in Cleveland Derek finally played the way we had expected. But after he got hurt Bernie just set his mind that there was no way he was going to keep Derek."

It was, Cooper concedes, difficult enough to be in charge of a team when it's winning. But when things go bad, then the pressures of sport are immeasurable. Fail to win a case for a client, and only the jury knows about it. But fail to put out a winning team and thousands of fans, the newspapers, television, and radio blurt out the bad news. It soon creates a hostility on the part of those in sports—it's "we" and "they." The "they" are the fans and the media, the outsiders daring to comment on the team.

"It takes a special kind of personality to remain in the world of sports, where there's lots of fantasy," says Cooper. "It's sometimes difficult dealing with players, who are different from the people you meet in the business world. Athletes are used to being catered to and having a fuss made over them."

Brown, apparently, didn't quite see it this way. He reportedly told a friend that he had made a million by sweating, and no young kid was going to take it away.

"Brown's first order of business was to unload his biggest headache—Derek Sanderson," says one of the many ex-Blazers. "Derek really busted a gut getting ready. He wanted this very badly. He begged and pleaded with them to let him play. But Watson and Brown said no." Derek himself recalls telling Watson he wanted to play soon, but Watson kept telling him, "just a little while longer."

So Derek continued to wait. As Derek remembers his hoped-for return to the Blazers, he began working out by himself. The club was on the road and Derek used the big empty arena, alone at center ice. Sometimes workmen would watch him. They'd sit on the stage, four or five of them, puffing cigars, cradling their coffee cups, and watching the world's most expensive athlete doing stops and starts, wind sprints, testing himself against himself. There was no competition, merely a shadowy goal and the remembrance of that last game, when he had scored against Cheevers and had said to his old buddy, "nothing to it." Perhaps, just perhaps, this whole thing could be salvaged after all. He didn't know that Brown was telling a friend that he "had made $50 million" and he knew how to be tough.

It was odd. For the first time in his life Derek was totally alone. Bob Woolf was in Boston. McKenzie had his own problems, returning off the broken arm, and losing his coaching post. The press had quietly begun to forget about Derek. All he had now was his car and his hotel suite. His moods would soar and then drop. "I'm still the best player in this league, next to Hull," he would say, and the next moment he would have his doubts whether it was all worthwhile.

"I don't know what the hell I'm going to do," he admitted one day. "I don't know when I can return. I don't know whether they'll let me. I got the feeling they're playing with my head. I'm not sure where all this will end." For the first time he began to strongly contemplate a return to the Bruins and imagined what it would be like. True, the Bruins weren't the same. They had lost a good chunk of their heart, players who had been there through the bad times and the good.

He came across Hull, who had been working at a fever pitch to make this new league go. Hull had appeared in virtually every WHA city whenever a new player was signed. He was the showcase and he was being paraded around. He had made dozens of appearances in North America to spread the word about the league. Now he was playing, and playing hurt. He had bone chips in an elbow and sore knees—but he was sticking it out.

"Derek, you've got to work hard," he told Sanderson. "Even though I'm your opposition I'm trying to give you good advice. Get up for it, for the sake of the team. But remember, you've got to do the right thing by this league."

Sanderson told him that he was seriously thinking of leaving, that suddenly it was no longer fun in Philadelphia.

"You've got to be happy wherever you play," acknowledged Hull, "and I know you're not happy here. But remember, if you were in Boston you wouldn't have got this much money." Then Hull gave him a final bit of advice: "If you've got to leave, then get out with as much money as you can. But get out with class."

One morning, as usual, Derek was working out alone. That's when he discovered a gang of young tough teen-agers he would nickname his "under the hill gang." One of the more bizarre times of his life was about to begin, when his only friends would be some street urchins from South Philadelphia—the wrong side of town.

"I was shooting the puck into the empty net," relates Derek. "It hit the post and went up into the stands. I didn't think anyone was even sitting up there. But there were two dead-end kids about fourteen years old."

For the next week they and their friends were to be a part of his new life. His family and teammates weren't around. Instead, some boys who look, spoke, and acted as he did when he was the biggest wise guy in Niagara Falls, Ontario, suddenly appeared on the scene and transported him back in time. He began to live in two worlds. There was his $31,000 car and his massive suite. Then there was his involvement with these kids, society's stepchildren.

"Give me back the puck," he shouted to the boys in the stands.

"Uh, uh," screamed back one of them. "The puck goes in the stands, it belongs to the fan."

"Not in practice, for Christ's sake," shouted Derek.

Then for some reason he's not quite sure of, he asked them if they wanted to play with him.

"Sure," replied one of them.

"Well, where's your stuff," asked Derek.

"We stashed it," replied the boy.

"I knew there was something wrong right there," says Derek. "You don't 'stash' your own skates. You 'leave' them somewhere, maybe, but you don't 'stash' them. I figured out pretty quickly what they were talking about.

"Okay, what did you steal?" asked Derek.

"Nothing," replied the leader, whose name was Davey.

"Come on, for crying out loud—I'm no kid," answered Derek.

"Okay, we took some goalie equipment from the University of Pennsylvania."

"Hey, that's not a bad score. I'll tell you what I'll do. A friend of mine needs some goalie things. I'll give you a tenner for them."

Derek got dressed and he and the boys went to the railroad yard near the arena. The equipment was stashed in a deserted field. Then they went back to the rink. Derek went to a telephone, called the school, and told them where to find the equipment.

At last, Derek Sanderson had found something worthwhile to do. From the time he had first gone to Philadelphia he had thought that he was going to work with poor kids—not just poor, bad. "I've taken enough from the United States," he had said one day in the hospital. "Now it's time I started to repay something." But he didn't want to work with the socially acceptable charities, the ones with "the phoney liberals with a drink in one hand and a check in the other." He really thought he could save bad kids "because I can speak their language." It was a strange time for him to be doing it, when his own career and future was in flux and he didn't quite know what would happen the next day. He was feeling pretty miserable about things. He would read a comment by Watson that "Sanderson will have to work his way onto the team, it won't be handed to him" and he was confused. But now he wasn't back in Niagara Falls any more, and he couldn't just pile into a roadster and take off on a long quiet drive and think. He was a man with some responsibility, and he couldn't handle any of it. More and more, this whole thing was some sort of nightmare game he was playing. It was unreal, yet frightening, and he didn't know where any of it would end.

After calling the university, Derek found skates and sticks for the boys and they took the ice with him. They played "keep away"—in which Derek attempted to keep them away from the puck—and after one hour he was bruised from their sticks and punches. Then he brought them up to the Blazers' dressing room.

"Don't whip anything," Derek told them in their language. He meant that they shouldn't steal. Then he grabbed a dozen sticks from the equipment room and they all piled into his car.

"I took them to their block in South Philly," Derek says. "Well, the car stops and they open the windows and start screaming. From out of nowhere forty kids show up. Geez, I was getting a little worried about them scratching the car, you know, because they were trying to grab the sticks in the back seat." Derek shouted, "Hey, don't you kids have anything to play with?" They told him they didn't.

"Well, aren't you going to get something for Christmas?" he asked.

"Are you kidding?" answered one.

"Pile in," Derek commanded. And half a dozen of them got back into the car and they were off. Derek drove around until he found a sporting goods store. Christmas arrived early as Derek, in a burst of generosity, brought the collection of boys inside.

"I got them a bunch of Phil Esposito street-hockey pucks, then I bought some goalie gloves—three right, one left—then footballs, softballs, basketballs. It must have come to about two hundred bucks. I opened my wallet and I guess I had about $800 on me. The kids couldn't believe it. Their eyes bugged open."

Then one of the youngsters said to Derek, as he handed him a piece of paper, "You'll have to sign a note."

"Sure," replied Derek. "I'll give you my autograph."

"Shit, I don't want your autograph. I want a note so when I take this stuff home my father won't think I stole it."

So Derek wrote: "Dear Sir, your son did not steal any of this stuff. I gave it to him as a gift because he's a good kid. [signed] Derek Sanderson."

The next day fifteen kids showed up and they played for two hours and Derek's team lost by 22-17. It kept up this way for awhile and finally the big team was home and Derek brought in his new friends to meet the Blazers.

"I wasn't worried about having them meet the players. These kids disciplined themselves. Sure, they were kids that had got into some scrapes. I think they even went to some kind of school for truants. People didn't think they could be handled. But anyone with an ounce of decency in them can handle kids like that. Just give a crap for them."

There was a new boy in the group and he started to stare at something near Lacroix's locker. Davey went over to the boy and smacked him across the back of his head. Soon, remembers Derek, Watson arrived and said, "Okay, you punks—out." Sanderson objected but Davey said, "That's okay, we're used to this kind of treatment."

"These kids were so poor," relates Derek, "that every time I saw them they were wearing the same clothes. One of them got stabbed by his father after he jumped in when his father was beating up his mother. So every day I'd drive them home in the Rolls and I knew they were skipping school, but I figured this was more important than any school could ever be."

One night Derek decided to take them to a game— it was stick night. "I told Watson I wanted to bring in the kids and he told me no. Shit, the place only had about 2,000 people. I figured screw him. I gave Dave about $150 and asked him to buy everyone an $8.50 seat. The kids bought the seats and when they went in a guard stopped them. Davey told him, 'out of my way, here's my ticket' and the guard was dumbstruck."

Buying those tickets was very important to Derek. He figured that buying the tickets would make the Blazers look like jerks. He was going to show them. Yet, he can't quite explain exactly what he was proving and who he was trying to prove it to. All he knew was that the top-price ticket he had bought would embarrass someone. That was very important to him—to make sure someone knew that he could spend what he wanted to, and didn't need any handouts.

There was someone missing from the group that Derek had bought tickets for—the boy whom Davey had smacked. The youngster indeed had coveted something of Lacroix's—tickets. He was outside the arena scalping them for $2 apiece. As the other boys filed in they were asked if they wanted free sticks—it was stick night. "Derek gives us real ones," Davey replied. "We don't need your cheap sticks."

The next day Derek was practicing again and someone handed him an official-looking form from the city. He was asked to sign it. If anything happened to the boys while they were playing, the city would not accept responsibility—Derek would. He claims that he went to the "front office" and told them, "What kind of crap is this? You've never been on a tough street. You never grew up like this." But that only killed it. It was over. He had to tell the boys that he couldn't sign the paper, that "I know you wouldn't want to sue me, but if your old man saw that you got injured he'd sue for fifty grand. That would be his way out, don't you see."

"That's okay," Davey replied, "There's always a jerk who screws things up for you."

Derek showed up at the rink on a Friday night. It was raining and the guards had kept Davey and his friends outside. Derek hadn't seen them for a few days and figured he wouldn't come across them again.

"Here," said Davey, thrusting a watch at Derek. "It's for Christmas."

He was quick to add: "We didn't steal nothing. We all chipped in."

"Where'd you get the money, though?" asked Derek.

"Oh, that," said Davey. "Well, anyway, we got you the watch so you shouldn't be late for practice."

"Now I'm going to get dressed for my first game back," relates Derek. "But Watson said don't get dressed. I asked him what he meant and he asked if I spoke to the doctor. I told him I had, that the doc said I could play if I felt okay."

"You're going to be embarrassed if you don't take off the uniform," said Watson.

"The doctor came in," says Derek. "He hemmed and hawed and said, 'I don't think they want you to play.' I asked him why not and he told me, 'I don't think they want to pay you.'

"You mean they want to get rid of me?" asked Derek.

"I think so," replied the doctor. "I think you're well enough to play, but they said I shouldn't let you."

Sanderson was "confused—the players were upset, the trainer didn't know what the hell was going on. The doctor was in the next room and everybody was running out. I had no one to turn to. So I went to McKenzie and he just shook his head and said, 'Derek, I don't know what they're trying to pull, but it's out of my hands now.'"

A former Blazer remembers vividly what life was like for Sanderson, and the events that led to the inevitable breakup.

"You know, the guys on the team never resented Derek's money. I don't know why he feels like that. I remember that he really did everything he could to try to be one of the guys. Once in Ottawa he called all the guys into the dressing room and said we should all get together, talk for a while. Then he sent out for Chinese food and the bill was like $95 and he paid for it. That was the type of guy he was. He never asked for anything back.

"But management resented the money. I think that Brown was against him from the start. Brown worked so hard for his money he couldn't believe that someone would come along and make that kind of money. And it bothered Brown that he had to pay Derek while Derek was in the hospital, and that only 3,000 people were coming to the games after Cooper had told Bernie that Derek would fill the place. Brown did everything to get rid of Derek.

"We started winning and Brown must have figured: 'Do we need him or don't we?' I think they were trying to make life rough for him so he'd quit."

The player recalls that often there would be a practice on a Monday, following a Sunday game. "They'd put the names of the guys on the board—guys who they wanted to work out on Monday—and they were rookies from the Eastern League. And Derek's name. And then after practice, when most of us left the ice, only the rookies were left—along with Derek. You just don't do that sort of thing to someone from the NHL. An old pro knows how much he's got to work to get back in shape. Derek had pride. But all they were doing was embarrassing him by singling him out. They lumped him along with a bunch of rookies. I'm convinced they were trying to see whether Derek would come back and answer them—you know, refuse to obey an order. Then they would have a reason to break his contract."

The player believes "definitely" that all this came on "orders from Brown. I know that Phil didn't care much for Derek, but I don't think he would have treated him this way unless he was under pressure. He knew that Derek would have enough pride in himself to work out without being singled out. Derek wasn't the type who would say, 'I'm getting two and a half million dollars.'

"I remember the last time Derek suited up for us. Brown had been trying to prove we could win without Derek, that we didn't need him at all. Most of us were confused about what was happening. We kept reading about Derek in the papers and we'd see things on television and no one understood the situation. There was just so much talk. Anyway, Derek suited up and Watson said something like 'You're not playing.' Then Derek asked why and Watson replied, 'Don't ask me.'

"I asked Derek what the hell was going on and he said, 'I don't know any more than you do. All I know is that they call me into the office every day, make me show up, and then don't tell me anything. I want to play and I can't play. Every time I want to do something they tell me I can't.'

"And you know something? I don't think Derek did know. It was all too bad. That game he got hurt against Cleveland was the best game he ever played for us. I think he would have liked Philadelphia. It was a matter of getting used to. And he didn't have enough time to do it."

"He treated his players like truck drivers," recalls a former Blazer employe about Brown. "Once he went into the dressing room and told the players, 'If I had to screw someone to get my way, I screwed him.' We had a good press basically, but he told the writers, 'Embarrass the players if you have to.' "

By now Brown and Cooper were on the verge of splitting. Cooper knew exactly what Brown was attempting to do to Sanderson. Derek knew it, too.

"While I was out they wanted me to punch a clock, to make me jump. I had to show up for all the games. I couldn't leave the building till the game was over. I had to go in the dressing room at the end. Parent, though, could do whatever he wanted to do. The day after he broke his foot, he wrapped his foot in a plastic bag and went hunting."

The Parent situation was strange, not quite so bizarre as Sanderson's, but worth some reflection. The goalie's lawyer was Howard Casper, a Philadelphian, who kept a very close watch on his star client.

"Casper was a combination general manager—p.r. man," claims an ex-Blazer. "It wasn't unusual to see Casper coming into the executive offices and giving advice about how his goalie should be played. I remember once Watson asked Bernie how he was feeling and Bernie told him he was fine. So he played the next night. But then Casper came in and said 'I think he's tired and shouldn't play.' I mean, I never heard of a player's lawyer ever giving advice on how to use the player."

While Brown and Watson bad-mouthed Derek constantly, and the Cooper-Brown situation headed for a showdown, Derek was in a state of minor hysteria.

"Christ, I'd be reading all the time about how I wasn't good enough to make the club, and how they were telling the press that I was lazy, things like that. I honestly believe they wanted me to crack. I think they wanted me to get to the point where I'd punch one of them in the mouth. Then they could suspend me and save $2,000 a day by not paying me."

"That's just what they want you to do," Woolf told him.

"I believe strongly that Brown was scared Derek wouldn't be able to return because of the injury—and that they'd have to pay him for the remainder of the contract," says Woolf. "So once Derek left the hospital, they tried to show that Derek had other things bothering him—prior conditions they weren't aware of. If they could establish this, then they thought they might have been able to beat the whole contract."

Woolf had to get Derek back to Boston, but under no circumstances did he want Derek to jump the team. As luck would have it, the Blazers were going to play in Boston again.

Events were quickly coming to a head now. Woolf asked Brown if it was okay for Derek to stay in Boston at his house, instead of at the team hotel. Brown agreed. Derek left Philadelphia for Boston with the Blazers and went to Woolf's house. He never returned to Philadelphia.

"The first thing I did when I got Derek home was to call up three different orthopedic surgeons," says Woolf. "I called up some pretty important men, like

Dr. Carter Rowe, the fellow who operated on Orr's knees. I took Derek from one doctor to the other—and let me tell you, you just can't make last-minute appointments that easily with a big surgeon. And all of them gave Derek a clean bill of health, and they said he was ready to play again. I wanted that. Then I told Brown that three doctors gave Derek a clean bill of health." With this as a wedge, Woolf and Sanderson resolved that they now would fight Brown, and that they were leaving the team under honorable conditions. As they saw it, no contract had been breeched on their part. Indeed, it was Philadelphia that refused to live up to the deal by not playing him. Once the surgeons had examined Derek, he was finished as a Philadelphian.

"You know," says Cooper wistfully, never for a moment bitter, "One of the sad things was that I never got the chance to see McKenzie and Sanderson play on the same line together."

Cooper was bought out by Brown and Brown installed an old friend, 38-year-old Dick Olson, as president. Fittingly, he joined the club after serving as an executive for the American Hospital Supply Corporation.

The events of the next few months are tangled, and the truth probably lies somewhere between the web of charges and counter-charges that were hurled by all sides.

There was, for example, the state of the Blazers. "We were priced wrong," says Olson, "at $1 more than the Flyers. This was ridiculous. I changed the prices to a more realistic level." Olson soon realized, however, that there was no way for the Blazers to make money— even if they filled the place and didn't have Derek's contract to contend with.

"We couldn't see our way clear with only 8,000

seats and a professional hockey payroll," explains Olson. "Even though we could see better times ahead, a better team, you couldn't make money in that situation if you played to capacity."

But headache number one was the Sanderson affair, and Olson's first official act (after chopping the prices) was to visit Derek. Woolf had told Olson he would fly Derek to Miami to meet with him, but he thought that it was simply a formality. The only way Derek would return to Philadelphia, said Woolf, would be under the existing contract. Olson, however, wanted to convince Sanderson to return and sign a new deal for less money. Brown had been phoning Woolf and telling him that Derek's salary was killing the club.

"Let me have a last crack at Derek," Olson told Woolf.

Brown, Cooper, Sanderson, and Woolf met. Some sort of novel carrot-and-stick approach was used to woo the player back. "Derek acts like a punk and no punk is going to take my money," Brown told Woolf. Olson, though, told Derek, "Get your ass on a plane and come back. It's not too late."

But it was. Derek refused. Now it wasn't the money any more that was the overriding concern. All he could think of was Boston, and it was where he wanted to be.

"We hoped to be able to salvage it," says Olson. "We had a few days off and there would be time for Derek to return and work himself into shape. But if we couldn't get him back, we were ready to contend that he had some prior conditions that had prevented him from playing. There was his colitis and his bad knees. Management said that these things existed prior to the contract and that these injuries prevented him from playing."

If indeed there were several prior injuries that prevented Derek from playing, why was management so anxious to get him back?

In any event, Derek was adamant. He did not want to return to Philadelphia. "We had some heated discussions about that," concedes Olson.

By now, everyone realized that Derek wasn't coming back—not to Philadelphia, at any rate. A friend had picked up the Rolls and driven it to Boston. That was where Derek really wanted to be.

Okay. Now everyone had to find a way out of the complex contract, a series of papers so extraordinary that to this day everyone involved cannot tell you exactly what the terms were. You hear them say: "Uh, I think it was $250,000 a year after three . . . no, after five . . . no, after five he would get less." Or: "There were bonuses for goal-scoring." Or: "No bonuses for goal-scoring, only if the club finished first or second." Or: "I heard he gets $400,000 the first year and the rest is all screwed up." Tied up in all this were Harold Sanderson's salary, the loan, the use of a car, and, perhaps, an inflation rider. Who knows?

One thing Woolf knew, though: He had a legitimate contract. His client didn't renege. Doctors could attest to the fact that no prior condition hampered him with the Blazers. Now, they were trying to get out of it. But it would cost them. What would a fair settlement be? As much as possible, of course.

Any settlement would include Harold Sanderson, naturally. Derek's father had been leading an interesting life. He single-handedly covered the entire province of Ontario—more than 400,000 square miles.

"I got off all the days I could manage from my regular job," he explains. "I had to keep that job, right?

This league was just beginning, and I wasn't going to blow a lifetime job down the drain just because some clown says he's got a hockey team going."

Harold explained to Watson that he had this other job, and even though Harold was the world's highest paid scout he still didn't want to give up the job that had paid the bills for all these years. Watson replied, "Fine, you just cover the games when you can."

Harold was having a fine old time. He was pleased as punch. His only son was on top of the world, and he had even provided for his old man. Harold always knew that Derek would amount to something. Oh, sure it had bothered him when his boy had been the third-line center all those years with Boston. But he knew deep down that the reason Derek was playing with second-string wingers was because the big name centers didn't know how to handle these guys. Derek, he knew, was smart enough to play with anyone. He wasn't a cry-baby, always looking to the averages, always worrying about fattening up his own statistics. Harold believed his son was the third-line center because he was the only one good enough not to play with high-scoring wings. Even when he was a junior, hadn't Hap Emms told young Derek that he would have to skate with so-and-so because the number one center couldn't do the job with so-and-so. And Harold remembers that Derek had seventeen different right and left wingers with him in the NHL, and he never had the time to get accustomed to them. Esposito had played with only three different wings on the Bruins, while Fred Stanfield, who anchored the number two line, had had to adjust to only four. Harold was just aching for Derek to get his chance in the number one spot. His dream would have been realized. But as time went by with

Philadelphia he started to wonder if his son would return.

Caroline Sanderson had not quite comprehended the whole thing from the beginning. She was born in Fife, Scotland, into "just a plain ordinary everyday working family." She had met Harold during the war, and came over here as his war bride. When Derek signed with Philadelphia, it was simply unreal.

"I still couldn't believe I was the mother of the world's richest athlete," she says. "I'm kind of a fundamentalist but still I thought, oh, my goodness. It always seemed like it wasn't really happening. But I guess it did."

It took her quite a while to realize she was awake. Even now, talking about it, she stutters: "How could anyone . . . so much money . . . it was just a little bit beyond belief . . . it was just too much to even realize . . . you never really imagine that much money."

Mrs. Sanderson was always the sort to see the bright side of things, yet when something of this magnitude occurred she just couldn't quite grasp it. She had always wanted Derek to finish high school, but when he made his decision to quit, she accepted it—even though she had always felt that "with a little application" Derek could have been a really super student.

She always believed he was mature for his age, and ultimately she had realized that "with his mind wandering, you know, what was going to be happening in the game tonight, what happened last night, it was pretty hard to concentrate on school. He really thought of nothing else but the love of the game."

During the winters, she recalls, he didn't have much time for girls. In the summers there was, well yes, some time. She had stopped reading "those things they were saying about my boy." It had bothered her too much. "I guess we all have our own image of someone," she says. "And that's not my image of Derek. I just prefer not to believe some of those things. As long as he calls me up, then I'm okay. He's a good boy. He calls, you know, and he always lets us know where he is and how he's doing."

He called while he was in the hospital in Philadelphia. Yes, Harold was upset that his son was sick. "But I told Derek that he had to do the job, and he had to do it right. And he told me, 'Dad, I'm upset. All this money they're paying me and I land up here in the hospital.' "

Harold started to get upset about the whole Philadelphia situation. Not that he had been ecstatic about it from the start.

"I told them from the beginning I was going to scout my own way, and give them reports in my own way," says Harold. He covered five or six games a week, almost all of them on weekends. When he first met Watson, he had been given "stupid forms I didn't agree with." What kind of forms? "Asinine scouting report forms. Like, does a guy drink, does he fool around with women? Is he reliable. This kind of crap. I made up my own form and they accepted it."

Then Watson wanted the reports every week. For the whole Ontario Hockey Association. For the hundreds of boys who would be eligible for drafting. Harold couldn't believe it.

"I had no one working for me," he explains. "So I told them I'd give them the reports in stages. Hell, you can't tell a player from week to week. You have to do it in selected stages, from time to time during the season."

He would go to Toronto, or Oshawa, or St. Catherines. Once he even made it as far as the Soo. "I thought it was a great job. But my wife, she didn't appreciate it much."

Harold's forms, he thought, were concise, intelligent, and clear. He wrote this about the highly regarded Denis Potvin, the number one player chosen by the NHL: "Good stand-up defenseman. Hits hard. Doesn't waste motion. Good puck carrier. Gets the puck out. Cool. Clever. MY KIND OF HOCKEY PLAYER. Dirty if necessary."

As Harold, in his fashion, beat the bushes in his 400,000 square-mile territory, he had one thought. "I looked for the things in a player that I had looked for in Derek when my boy was young."

He continued to go on his weekend excursions even while Derek was laid up, and even into December, when he realized what was going on with the Blazers. "I never wanted to intrude on him," says Harold. "Even when Derek was in the juniors and that old bastard Emms wasn't using Derek the way he should have, I never interfered. I figured, okay, Derek has that hassle with Cooper to settle, but I had my job to do."

The Blazers had turned down the only player that Mr. Sanderson provided them with—Cottringer. "That," claims Harold, "was where interference from Brown came in. You know, that Brown—he didn't strike me from the beginning. Cooper was a nice enough guy. But Brown, he was strictly money. And he thought that made him a hockey executive, for Christ's sake. That's why Cottringer played only two games—because Brown said so. But I guess if the s.o.b. has that much money, he's got a right to say what he wants to."

Derek came home for Christmas for a few days and his mother and father could sense that he seemed to have things on his mind that he couldn't resolve. But they were going to let him work it out by himself.

"Sure it bothered me," says Harold. "The way they treated him. He's the end of the world to me, you know. They never gave him the chance. He could have made that league go. He's got the personality for it."

By the time it all was over, Harold Sanderson didn't want any more to do with the Blazers. He had sent his employers a total of two scouting reports in the five months. "They take a hell of a long time to do right," he explains.

Now, though, Derek would be rid of the Blazers. Harold thought that finally his boy would go somewhere his talents would be appreciated. "I think it's going to be bloody great," said Harold. "He's going to show everybody in both leagues what it's all about."

Before signing anything, though, Woolf knew he had to make Derek a free agent. After some heavy talking to the league, he received an agreement that if he could settle the contract with the Blazers, Derek could do what he wanted—negotiate independently with anyone. He wouldn't be bound to the WHA or to the Blazers. And so Brown, Olson, and Woolf hammered out the details. There was some cursing and fuming at first but at the end, Olson recalls, "we settled it all very peacefully."

It cost the Blazers about $800,000 to get out of Derek's contract. More than $600,000 would go directly to Derek. The rest was part settlement on Harold Sanderson's contract and other intertwined expenses that had gone into the original deal. Thus, Derek Sanderson left Philadelphia and had the honor of becoming history's highest paid player on the basis of goals scored—more than $250,000 a goal.

seven

WOOLF was attending President Nixon's Inaugural when the Chicago Cougars of the WHA attempted to reach him. Only half the season remained. The Cougars were a comfortable last in the Western Division and were the only team that had a losing record at home. They offered Derek $100,000 to finish playing out the season for them. Not only that, when the campaign was over, he would be a free agent with no ties to the club. Since the Cougars weren't going to make the playoffs, Derek had to play only another nine weeks to earn his six figures.

Harry Sinden of the Bruins also called. "I told Bob that he damn well better remember us if Derek was going to another club," recalls Sinden.

Then the Raiders contacted Woolf. They were a club in flux, being run by the league until a new ownership could be put together. The original owners, a pair of New Jersey lawyers named Dick Wood and Sy Siegel, who happened to be hockey fans, had optimistically underestimated the start-up costs for a New York team in a new league. At times, the crowd couldn't even pay the $17,000 Madison Square Garden rental fee.

But a huge group of businessmen was interested in buying the club, and it included the son of the board chairman of the J. Walter Thompson advertising agency, one of the world's largest.

"We can make Derek one of the most important men in America," they told Woolf. "Sanderson could be packaged, and with the exposure in New York and the resources of J. Walter Thompson, he can become a millionaire." They offered Derek about $200,000 a year to come to New York. Not only that, they would make him a partner in the club—making Derek the only hockey player who would own a piece of the team he played for.

As far as the Bruins were concerned, though, Sanderson still belonged to their league. They even sent out telegrams warning other NHL clubs not to talk to Derek or Woolf about rejoining the league with anyone other than Boston. That would be considered tampering. In fact, however, Derek was a free agent. If his NHL contract had been valid he would have remained a Bruin. Still, the NHL had decided to act toward all jumpers as if they remained their property. This didn't stop three NHL clubs from contacting Woolf and asking if Derek were available for about $200,000 a year.

"But I was hamstrung because I couldn't go out and negotiate for Derek on any of these offers," explains Woolf. "Derek decided he only wanted to be with Boston so what was the sense of exploring any of these offers further?"

Woolf, a realist, realized that he and Derek would have to revise their thinking on money. The $200,000 offers coming in were for real—but was it good enough? It had taken, after all, more than $2.5 million to get Derek lured away from the Bruins and the NHL. A miserly $200,000 wasn't good enough then, and it might not be good enough now. On the other hand, just what was Derek worth?

Woolf knew there was no way the Bruins were going to be talking about $200,000 annually—even though the club had got burned previously by not meeting higher demands. Derek had received about $50,000 from the Bruins the year before. He wanted to go back— for more, of course—but he was willing to take less than the money he had lately become accustomed to. Luckily, the Bruins needed him.

Indeed, the day after Sanderson had settled his Blazer contract, the Bostonians suffered one of the most embarrassing defeats in their history. They lost to the lowly New York Islanders by 9-7. The Islanders were on their way to compiling the most losses in league history. That victory was to be one of only twelve for the Islanders—equalling a record low.

No one knew it then, but that Islander victory marked the end of the Bruins' chances for first place, and the beginning of their search to land Derek Sanderson. The Bruins had finished first in the East Division the previous two seasons. They were the Stanley Cup winners two of the previous three years. But now their basic weakness was showing. True they had Orr and Esposito, and no one could match that. But they had lost defensive strength. Their goaltending was poor with Cheevers gone. That spark that had flared when they were losing in a game, when they had the feeling that no matter how far behind they'd be they could always come back, was being extinguished. Before the season Espo-

sito had spoken of the team's lost feeling of "together-
ness" and how it would return this time. But he didn't
anticipate the toll the defections would take. Esposito
believed that the guys would be "pulling harder" after
McKenzie, Cheevers, and Derek had left. He had a vague
hope that the club's slow disintegration as a family—
which had started even before the leavings because of
each player's many outside interests—would suddenly
halt and it would be like old times again. There would be
the so-called Big Bad Bruins on the ice again, a rough-
and-tumble, fun-loving collection of players who were
stunned by a defeat much as the heavyweight champion
would be surprised if a featherweight knocked him down
with a left hook.

The coach of this team was the affable Tom Johnson, a bow tie-wearing, pipe-smoking man who often
spoke of the absurdity of his situation.

"I hope they'll listen to me when I have a practice,"
he would say. There was a twinkle in his eye, but truth
on his lips. He appreciated the fact that the team was a
championship squad, and it had been successful despite
its cavalier attitude toward curfew and off-limits places.
Oh, sometimes—when the team might lose a game or be
tied by a nonentity—Johnson would shake things up a
little. But for the most part he allowed the players to
relax in workouts. He knew they could indeed turn it on
when they had to. The players appreciated this. Esposito
even confessed that "sometimes I feel sorry for Tom. He
really lets us get away with murder." So long as the club
won, though, everyone was happy.

The players never felt as passionately toward Johnson as they had toward Sinden, the man who had quit as
coach after leading them to their first Stanley Cup in
twenty-nine years in 1970. Sinden had been part of

them, a young, intense leader who had taken over the club when it was in last place and led them out of the wilderness. Under him they established the reputation as hockey's best brawlers, a club that for no reason (apparently) would pick a fight and wouldn't stop until it had won. Sinden never quite admitted that his team was dirty, or even rough. "How come no one ever complained when we were last?" he wanted to know, or he'd say, "We're not rough. We just stand up for our rights." And the players loved him.

Sinden had been coach for only one year when Derek first joined the team. The pair, according to Derek, "dug each other." Derek claims that he once saved Sinden in the minors, after an opponent headed for the players' bench and was about to take on the coach. Derek stepped in and mopped up things.

The pair got on famously. When Sanderson first reported to camp in 1967 Sinden told him, "You probably won't make the team."

"How the hell would you know?" Sanderson shot back. "You're full of shit."

"Well, Derek made the team and I guess he thought I was some kind of jerk for judging him like that," says Sinden.

The Bruins were floundering after that incredible defeat to the Islanders. They were confused, uncertain where they were going. In a matter of two weeks they went from a contending position, in second place only five points behind Montreal, to third place and thirteen points back. This was a highly unaccustomed spot for the Bruins, a club that had finished no lower than second for the previous four years.

Sinden was the managing director of the team. He had rejoined them five months before in a dramatic homecoming. He had quit after winning the 1970 Stanley Cup because the Bruins had offered him only a $2,000 raise. In the 2½ years in between he had been an executive with a home construction company, a fitting job since his boisterous Bruins had been one of history's great wreckers. But his company went bankrupt. During his years wearing a white shirt and tie he had entertained thoughts about returning, but only when Boston contacted him did he become really interested. First, though, was the Team Canada business. He was the coach and stayed with the team through July, August, and September. Then, in early October, he rejoined the Bruins—as head of the whole operation.

It was strange that he was returning to a club that just a few years before hadn't wanted to give him more than the equivalent of a $40 a week raise for winning the cup—and now he was the overseer of the hockey operation.

"I think the Bruins' ownership realized there was a changing of the guard, so to speak," explains Sinden. "Hockey had to change with the times. The changes in hockey were dramatic, drastic, and imminent. And they told me they needed someone who was willing and flexible enough to change, and to respect the changes. I guess they wanted someone who wasn't too Establishment." Sinden was only forty years old when he returned to Boston.

"Of all the players I had with me in Boston in 1970, Derek and Cheevers were the ones I knew I was going to miss most," relates Sinden. "I figured Derek was gone for ten years, though, and I didn't think about getting him back. But I could have used him. He was a bona fide NHL center—an excellent face-off man, a good penalty killer. Oh, you can get guys with those qualities, sure.

But it takes a while before they really fill those roles. But Derek also added a little pizazz—which I've always felt a team needs. So I knew we'd miss him. And we did."

When Sinden read in the newspapers about Derek's settlement with the Blazers—reportedly for $1 million—he reached for the telephone to call Woolf. Sinden had no hesitation about getting Derek back. He knew what he could do and what he could mean to the club. But Sinden also realized that he had rejoined the Bruins after Derek had left, and Sinden hadn't been around during the long negotiations. He didn't have a feel for the dynamics of the situation, and didn't know how the players would react to their former teammate.

"If there was animosity or ill feeling, I certainly didn't have it," says Sinden. "I wanted Derek Sanderson, the hockey player and personality I knew in 1970—I wanted him back because I knew he could help us.

Sinden was in a position of supreme power on the club, answerable only to young Adams. And even Westy had hired Sinden with the understanding there would be no interference. Sinden, in effect, was given carte blanche. If he wanted Derek back, Derek would come back. Perhaps, though, there was one man who had to approve—"Mr. Adams, Sr."

Sinden called Woolf and told him he was interested in seeing Derek, but before they could even talk contract Derek would have to come back from Miami and work out in front of Sinden to his satisfaction. In a sense, Sinden was asking hockey's highest priced talent to audition.

"You don't buy a house until you walk through it," Sinden explained.

This was what Derek had been waiting for. He immediately flew to Boston after Sinden told him that, if things worked out right, negotiations would start where they left off when Derek had jumped.

Sinden watched from the stands as Sanderson took the Boston Garden ice following a practice by the Braves, the Bruins' American League farm team. Sanderson was alone except for Armand (Bep) Guidolin, the Braves' coach.

In his years as coach of the Bruins, Sinden had devised a little ten-minute test to determine how far along his players had been during training camp. He would test them after six days to see whether they were progressing. He sent Derek on wind sprints across the Garden ice—195 feet long. Back and forth went Derek, sixty yards at a clip. Sinden was watching how his pupil would do at the end, to see "how well he handled the last two or three."

The next day he tested Derek again. Derek believed he had genuinely surprised Sinden, that his ex-coach "thought I was in really good shape." Sinden concedes now that "it was a little better than I expected, but he was almost as far away as I expected."

The second workout was over and Sinden was worried. He wanted to know just how the other Bruin players felt about Derek and his possible return.

"I told them I was thinking of signing Derek if he could get in reasonable shape and I asked their feelings. And everyone I spoke to just wanted some assurance that Derek was serious and was going to play hockey, that his primary interest in coming back to the team was to help the team. It was a legitimate question on their part—and mine, and anybody else who wanted to ask it. You see, here's a guy that's supposed to be coming back with $1 million. Everyone respected his playing ability. But they had questions about his motives."

Woolf, Sanderson, and Sinden began negotiations, an odd situation since 2½ years earlier Woolf had represented Sinden when Sinden dealt with management for more money. Now Woolf not only was representing Derek, he was also Milt Schmidt's lawyer, and Schmidt was the general manager of the club.

The money talks bogged down. In fact, Sanderson and Sinden had words and Derek came back to Woolf and told him he didn't think they could get together. Sinden wasn't offering much more than Derek had made the previous season. At the very least, Woolf had hoped the talks would start at about $90,000 a year.

"Funny about those talks," recalls Woolf. "Here's Derek, a guy who got all those millions from Philadelphia and in the end he didn't want it. He had a bad attitude about the thing from the start. And now he's talking about taking a cut in pay in the millions, and he'll have to make all sorts of sacrifices for less money, and he wanted it. It's hard to figure."

During the impasse, Woolf and Sanderson bided their time. It perhaps is unfair to say they were happy that the Bruins were doing so poorly on the ice. But they certainly knew that after each defeat, Derek Sanderson looked better and better.

Then one Saturday night Woolf and Derek were watching the Bruins play the Rangers on television in Derek's apartment. The Rangers were streaking, the Bruins were sinking. A Boston victory was a must. If the Rangers won, most people figured, they would lock up second place. The Bruins? They'd have to be content with third. The Rangers won—in fact they slaughtered the Bruins by 7-3.

When the last buzzer sounded, Woolf turned to Derek and said, "This is a good time to call Harry."

Sinden answered the phone in his Boston Garden office. "I'll come right over," he told Derek. When he arrived, Woolf and Sanderson found Sinden "down in the dumps," according to Woolf. He was upset at the way things had gone from the beginning—his return to Boston had been something less than heroic. But perhaps, just perhaps, he still could turn things around to the way he had remembered them.

The three of them stayed locked in Derek's apartment until 3 A.M. They "fought tooth and nail," recalls Woolf.

"Do you have the guts to stick it out?" Sinden asked Sanderson.

"Would you be willing to eat humble pie, not to mouth off to the press, not ruffle feathers? What are you going to think when some of the other guys don't accept you? What's your attitude?" There were these and other questions, and Woolf marveled at the way Sanderson fielded them, and that Sanderson would eat crow and would stuff his feelings. And again Woolf reflected on the irony: that they begged him to come to Philadelphia to make him a millionaire, but that now Sanderson would agree to terms for much less, and he would be coming back hat in hand. Through it all, though, Sinden maintained his respect for Derek.

"I liked him in 1970, and I liked him now," says Sinden. "A lot of people say he's changed, but I think that maybe he just got older, like everybody else. He's still the same basically: a little flamboyant. You overlook a lot with Derek. But behind it all, he's just what he says he is—a high school dropout."

Finally, they agreed on a deal. Derek would finish out the season and would also play next year. Woolf wanted a no-trade clause, but Sinden said he couldn't give him one, that the NHL wouldn't permit it. Woolf knew the Bruins were looking for a goalie and he was worried that perhaps the Bruins would take Derek back, sign him, and then suddenly trade him to Chicago or Oakland for a goaltender. "I can't put it in writing, but I'll give you my word that he won't be traded," said Sinden.

The deal that was signed, for 1½ years, was worth about $175,000. It was a substantial raise from what he'd been getting from the Bruins in the past. But it was equal to about five weeks' work with the Blazers.

When the three, bleary-eyed, ended the negotiations, Sinden told them the announcement would be made in a few days. It would be low-keyed, when the Bruins were on the road in Minnesota. This way there would be no big deal, no tension, no embarrassing questions.

But the next morning Sinden called Woolf and told him it wasn't a deal yet—the old man wanted to see Derek. Mr. Adams, Sr. was in Massachusetts General Hospital. He hadn't seen him since they had parted six months before.

"Mr. Adams claimed he had squatter's rights to Derek," recalls Sinden. "I guess he felt that he had saved Derek when he was a youngster, and kind of nursed him along. So I wanted Mr. Adams to talk to Derek. I wanted him to alleviate any doubts or fears in his head that Derek didn't want to play hockey any more, that he was just going to come back and screw around.

"Derek always thought a lot about Mr. Adams, and

the feeling was mutual. Mr. Adams was dying. He could hardly speak."

It was, recalls Woolf, "kind of like the prodigal son returning. Very dramatic. I don't really think there was any doubt about the contract in Harry's mind. I think it was simply that Mr. Adams wanted to see Derek again."

Adams and Sanderson joked about the things that had happened between them. Derek then explained the full story—the money, his injury, the quitting.

"You're not going to come and act like a big shot, are you, Sandy?" the old man asked. "Are you going to try?"

Sanderson said "yes," and how he had always wanted to be with the Bruins but that things happened, and that no twenty-six-year-old kid could ever turn down the offer that he had received.

"Now I understand," said Adams.

Woolf and Sanderson left and Adams whispered to Sinden, "Sign him."

"They said they wanted the old man to give his final approval," recalls Woolf. "But I surmise Mr. Adams just wanted to see Derek, to see whether it was the same kid that he had grown to love or whether that much money had changed Derek."

Meanwhile, the rest of the WHA was undergoing the expected first-year growing pains. If it seemed to the general public at times that the only one doing anything controversial was Derek, that was simply because, well, Derek was Derek. The other teams in the United States had no one like him. They couldn't get the newspaper space even for winning teams. Derek received ink playing for a team that won two games in its first six weeks.

There were some bizarre happenings on other clubs, though. Take the Alberta Oilers, based in Edmonton.' They played in the grandly named Edmonton Gardens, which had been built in 1906. It had been renovated once.

But to its flamboyant owner, Bill Hunter, the Gardens was a modern palace, a latter-day Taj Mahal where the world's finest hockey players would glide over the artificial ice and pirouette into the hearts of Albertans everywhere. What did it matter that the place held only 5,200 people? Some day, shouted Hunter, he would have a 17,000-seat arena. If the city didn't want to get one, why, he'd build it himself.

Hunter was the perfect choice for a man to lead a first-year team in a first-year league in a city with the smallest population base of any major league hockey club. "Every event was the greatest moment in sports history," says a colleague.

True, Hunter had some problems. In fact, he had lots of problems. The club averaged 3,800 fans a game. At a $6 top the whole season's gate receipts might, with luck, meet the payroll. Still, that was okay. He had expected to lose money the first year, and anyway the new building would be ready by year two.

The major problem was—Edmonton was just too damn far from anyplace else. The closest league city was Winnipeg—1,600 miles away. No other team in any other sport was as isolated as Edmonton. That created the most bizarre scheduling hockey had seen. It started, for example, with four road games in five nights. Then came a home stretch that saw the Oilers play five home games in seven days.

"It's just socially impossible to ask people to go to

five hockey games a week," moans one official. "I mean, would you buy season's tickets knowing that you had to commit yourself every night, even if you loved the game? You never saw so many tickets go to waste."

Because Edmonton was so far from other WHA cities, back-to-back games often were played against the same teams in Edmonton. This put the Oilers at a disadvantage in hawking tickets. If you saw Los Angeles on a Monday night, would you want to see them again on Tuesday?

The road schedule was equally strange. After a home stretch that saw Edmonton play Houston on Friday, Ottawa on Sunday, New York on Tuesday, Los Angeles on Thursday and Saturday, and Cleveland on Sunday, the next week Alberta was at Minnesota on Tuesday, Philadelphia on Wednesday, New England on Friday, New York on Saturday, Ottawa on Sunday, and Winnipeg on Tuesday.

So Edmonton became a great home team. But on the road the travel took its toll. The Oilers wound up the first season as the WHA's only winning team that lost twice as many road games as it won. It was understandable. The Vancouver Canucks put on more miles than any other team in the NHL—about 65,000. The Oilers traveled more than 100,000 miles.

Hunter saw only the sunshine. He was not only the club's executive vice president, but also the general manager and coach. "My life's savings are in this team," he would say, and he would attempt anything to make it go. If the press was less than kind after a bad game, he would berate them. He had been used to getting his own way in the town. After all, hadn't he packed the place for years when his Edmonton Oil Kings were the toast of junior hockey? Of course, the prices for the juniors were only half what they were now. He had lured back a lot of his former Oil Kings or players who had been brought up in the Edmonton area. His persuasiveness had convinced nine NHL'ers to jump to his new team.

If the fans were slow in coming, he jazzed it up. He called his games "A Carnival of Fun." He replaced the traditional organist—a fixture at hockey as much as the ice—with a fourteen-piece band. He gave away TV sets and ten-speed bicycles. Enthusiasm was what he wanted —and fans. An observer of the scene notes that Hunter was "the Charles O. Finley of the WHA. He was flamboyant. Being next to him was like standing near the right hand of God. He has a very high opinion of Bill Hunter and he must have been tough to work for. He felt no one could do it as well as Bill Hunter."

His players delighted in a little bit of comeuppance he experienced. Their plane was grounded by fog in some airport in North America and there was a long line of people complaining about the delay. Hunter shot to the front of the line, saw someone in a uniform, and said, "I'm Bill Hunter and I'm the owner of this team and we've got to get going." And the other man replied, "I'm Joe Smith and I'm with the U.S. government. Get back to the end of the line." Hunter, flushed, walked back and it must have seemed to him he was running the gauntlet as he passed his players, each of whom was giggling and cupping a hand over a mouth to conceal the grins.

While there was intrigue and zany happenings going on through the rest of the WHA, the New England Whalers calmly and thoughtfully put together the club that would win with the best record and capture the playoffs. Yet, the Whalers were to engage in one of the weirder events in the history of the sport when the long season was at an end, with naked players fighting some angry, drunk fans in Winnipeg.

The Whalers started to take shape over a glass of beer. Howard Baldwin, a young businessman whose hockey career was cut short when Coach Jack Kelley dropped him from the Boston University hockey team, had been thinking of putting up a rink in a Boston suburb. His partner was to be an ex-Harvard man, John Coburn. While discussing the problems of putting up a rink, the man who sold the refrigeration equipment asked if they had ever heard of this new hockey league called the WHA.

In a few months the pair had formed a corporation and now they looked for a man to head the club. Kelley was the logical choice. He was the most successful collegiate hockey coach in the United States. His teams had just won the National Collegiate Athletic Association championship for the second straight year. Kelley signed on as coach-general manager. In short order he snared ten players from the NHL, including former Bruins in Ted Green, Tom Williams, and Tom Webster. In addition, the New England flavor was enhanced when five players who had played for local college teams or were born in the area also were chosen.

There was no limitless supply of money, and Kelley stayed away from the superstars. Instead, he could buy three or four solid players for what one all-star would cost. This philosophy of team building obviously worked. Despite the best record in the league, no Whaler made the first all-star team.

Working with pros was a new experience for Kelley. He discovered to his delight that they didn't have to be continually motivated. They knew, for the most part, what they had to do. But Kelley wasn't prepared for the sort of travel big-league hockey must endure. "In the colleges," he explains, "we had games on Wednesdays and Saturdays. The biggest trip we took was a fifty-five-minute bus ride to New Hampshire." It took time for Kelley to realize that the travel and the long season would take its toll. By the end of the campaign he thought it was like an endurance test—who ever would remain standing would win.

Yet, there were benefits. He explains, "If I had an idea, something I thought was worthwhile, I only had to walk a couple of doors out of my office, into Howard Baldwin's office, discuss it with him and get a yes or no. If yes, you followed through. But in college if I came up with what I thought was a good idea I had to go to the director of athletics. He'd have to wait until the athletic council met. If they thought it was a good idea they'd send it over to the assistant to the president and eventually it might get to the president. If he liked it he took it to the trustees—and I'd find out two years later whether it was going to go through."

Green was one of his surprises. Known as "Terrible Ted" in his heyday with the Bruins, his days in the NHL had been numbered after his stick-swinging fight in a 1969 exhibition game that left him with a fractured skull that required several operations. Somehow, he had managed to return to hockey after sitting out a year. Green looked forward to the opening game. He felt he had to prove to the Bruins that they had given up on him too soon. The fact he scored in that game didn't hurt his ego any.

Because the team had its share of old pros, and a heady management, things progressed smoothly. Oh, there were the little oddities—such as discovering at 3 A.M. that there was no way for them to get to Boston for an afternoon game (they wound up aboard a 120-seat plane that was supposed to be deadheading for New York from Montreal). And there was the time that $15,000 worth of equipment was stolen the day before a game against Cleveland. Everyone on the club "played Sherlock Holmes," recalls Kelley. Some of the loot was recovered, but eleven players performed while wearing new skates. They wound up with pinched toes.

The finals, for the Avco World Trophy (the new league's Stanley Cup), was to produce the Whalers' most absurd moment. The club was at Winnipeg. In the final seconds, as the Whalers stormed around the Winnipeg goal in a desperate effort to tie the score, a fan reached over the sideboards and grabbed Green in a headlock. Green swung at the fan, missed, and the fan, whose florid face attested to more than one swig of beer, attempted to punch Green. But the game ended peacefully and the Whalers, losers, trudged off to the locker room.

But now was the time for the traditional naming of the three stars—and Canadians take these post-game honors very seriously. This was a special night. A little crippled boy was to make the presentations to the three outstanding players. No one had told the Whalers' Rick Ley, though, that he had been named the second star. Ley was in the dressing room, his skates off, in his underwear. Out on the ice the youngster in the wheelchair was ready to present the second-star award and the name "Rick Ley" was announced. No Rick Ley showed up. After five seconds some of the fans growled. Thousands started to boo. Someone rushed into the Whalers' room to tell Ley he had won the award, but he said he was undressed and couldn't accept it.

Within a minute several drunk fans pounded on the door to the locker room. There were no police around—

they were still busy trying to quiet the fan who had headlocked Green. One of the fans opened the door, shouted some obscenities, and shut it. Then, perhaps egged on by his friends, he shoved his way in. Kelley happened to be standing near the door. He swung at the fan and jammed his wrist. "Oh, my God," Kelly thought, "Now the wrist is no good and I'm wearing glasses. This guy is going to kill me." Kelley held on for dear life, simply hoping that the fan couldn't land a punch. Meanwhile, the club's third-string goalie, Bob Berglund, swung at someone—he broke his thumb.

By now the players realized this wasn't a post-game tirade by their coach. They leaped out at the fans and chased them onto the runway under the rink. And the crowd missed one of the best shows of the first WHA season: Eight naked players swinging at some drunk fans.

Southern California had as much claim to hockey as sunbathing in December had in the Yukon. For several years the National Hockey League had languished in Los Angeles, even though more than 600,000 ex-Canadians lived in the state. They managed to avoid the sport.

"I know why they left Canada," said the Los Angeles Kings' owner, Jack Kent Cooke. "They hate hockey."

That didn't stop the Los Angeles Sharks from opening in the Sports Arena. The club's president was Dennis Murphy, the league's founder. The coach was a screamer named Terry Slater, who had studied for his master's degree in child psychology. He had even taught slow learners how to read. He was sure he could teach hockey players how to skate.

Strange things happened in Los Angeles, of course.

They may be grouped under natural phenomena. Certainly, not even executives of the team can explain a series of events that happened to the Sharks. There was, first of all, the attendance. The Kings, with such clubs as Montreal and the Bruins to play host to, had averaged only 7,000 a game the season before. "I'll be happy to see 3,000 fans a game," said Murphy. Instead, the Sharks averaged 6,000.

There were no heroes on the team, no one individual the club could point to and say, "He's our biggest commodity. Let's package him."

But the Sharks did have a player with the magnificent name of Bart Crashley. He became, says one club official, "our Golden Boy. He was a good-looking guy who had played one season in the NHL, so he had some credentials. We got him on as many shows as we could. Why, we had him on 'The Dating Game.'" Crashley won a trip to Gilman Hot Springs.

Opening night surprised everyone in Los Angeles when 11,430 people showed up. That stunning attendance gave the club a sort of instant credibility.

Although attendance again rarely approached that figure it remained respectable despite a rather remarkable statistic: the Sharks were the only winning team in hockey that had a losing record at home. They had, in fact, the best road mark in the league. It didn't take much psychology for Slater to figure out the reason: his boys were Canadians, and they had found Hollywood.

"They just can't concentrate," he explained. "They're either in their pools, or friends come in to visit and they wind up going to Disneyland or Knott's Berry Farm." It is not an atmosphere conducive to playing hockey, to getting psyched and in a tough frame of mind.

Slater, at thirty-four younger than some of his players, came with a reputation as somewhat of a flake. There was the time in the minors, for example, when he came in to see his slumping team in the dressing room before a game. "Fellows, my father just died. I can't stay here, but win it for my old man," he told them. Then he left. Of course, they won. Of course, there was nothing in the world wrong with Slater's old man.

Although he wasn't happy about it, Slater could accept a defeat in somewhat good graces if he thought his fellows had tried hard. If he thought they had been dogging it, though, he simply would refuse to talk to them on the plane rides back home.

He wasn't afraid to try things. One night he had a dream that a defenseman of his named Gerry Odrowski played center. The next night he pulled Odrowski off the defense, planted him at center—and Odrowski scored the winning goal.

The unexpected, the unusual—these were the things southern Californians were enchanted with. There was even a television star or two at the games and one night Peter Graves of "Mission: Impossible" showed up. The search for fans took up much of management's waking hours. They thought of ways to lure them in. There was the newspaper advertisements showing the bald heads of three players and underneath was the copy: "Can you match this?" Every bald-headed man in Los Angeles was invited to the game for free. They received wigs dyed in purple or red or orange. Other nights lucky fans might get giant chocolate sundaes, or outsize pizzas or 3-foot-long heroes. Strangely, one of the promotions that bombed was all-Canada night. Every ex-Canadian was invited at a discount and was given a chicken dinner. It was one of the more disappointing crowds.

It shouldn't have seemed strange, then, when one day the Sharks announced that their next Sunday game was going to start at 11 o'clock in the morning. The announcement came on a Tuesday, with barely enough time to notify the ticket-holders. The game originally had been scheduled for 2 P.M., but since it was going to be televised into eastern Canada—where it was three hours later—maximum exposure mandated moving the game up. To entice the people, management offered free coffee and doughnuts to the early arrivals. It was, at best, a feeble gesture. Who would go to a hockey game at 11 o'clock on Sunday morning?

Sunday came—and the monsoon season had begun. Sheets of rain enveloped everything. The team's public relations director, Hank Ives, could hardly see the road as he drove to the game with his wife and said, "If we're lucky, the players' wives will be there today."

He was surprised when he saw a long line of fans for the coffee and doughnuts. And then beyond the parking lot he saw the beginnings of a massive traffic jam. They were coming to see the Sharks, for God's sakes.

That morning, 12,804 fans showed up. To this day no one can explain why. Perhaps, Ives suggests, "Maybe everyone thought they were going to church."

"We can laugh now about it, but some of the players' demands were ridiculous," says the Winnipeg Jets' general manager, Annis Stukus.

The Jets became the target for more outrageous salaries than anyone else in the new league simply because they had been the first to make a player a millionaire when they snared Hull. Of course, the million didn't come from Winnipeg's pocket. The league had chipped in. But still, the Jets were going to pay the Golden Jet a quarter of a million annually.

A player who was earning $22,000 a year from the NHL asked the Jets for $60,000—plus a $40,000 bonus for jumping. Another player said, "I played twenty-two games in the NHL—I'm worth $55,000."

"What hurt us were the reports of what other guys were supposed to be getting," explains Stukus. "Sure, we paid Bobby that money. But then the rumors went wild. Take Wayne Connelly, a good, solid NHL'er. When he jumped to the Minnesota Fighting Saints the press said he was getting $90,000. No way he was making that sort of money. But now the agents had got into this money thing, and you know that most agents are lawyers, and lawyers can't advertise for clients. So what do they do? They get a $50,000 contract for their boy, but then tell the media—off the record, of course—that the contract was worth six figures. That might be true, but for two years or three years. Anyway, this makes the lawyer look good and other players flock to him."

Hull drove himself to make the league go. When he finally was able to play, after different court rulings that confused him and his attorneys, his weight had fallen from 197 pounds to 182. He had been like a man possessed in his single-minded determination to associate himself with a viable operation. In a private crusade, he played thirty, thirty-five, even forty minutes a game, punishing himself despite leg and knee and arm injuries. In every city he attended he would sign autographs before games from the side of the rink, an unheard of gesture. While his teammates practiced, Hull would stand patiently near the protective glass while tiny hands shoved pieces of paper between the panes toward him. Afterwards, win or lose, he'd remain for thirty or forty minutes, again signing his name.

One Winnipeg observer remarks about Hull: "Here was a man who played fifteen years in the NHL. He was one of the few who was included in Russian books on hockey. But after fifteen years with Chicago, and all sorts of business ventures, he wasn't set financially. In one year we made him a millionaire. Why wouldn't he jump?"

Stukus had to hold Hull back "or he would have killed himself. I guess there was so much involved for him. Here was a waning superstar and suddenly he had a chance not only to be Mr. Big of an entire league, but to get rich at the same time."

The Jets were fortunate in several areas. Although they had spent a small fortune in acquiring Hull, they acquired no other front-line National League players among the forwards or defense. Thus, their payroll actually was kept within some sort of limits.

In Stukus they had one of the few WHA executives who had actually dealt with professional athletes before. He had started two Canadian Football League franchises—the Edmonton Eskimos and the B.C. Lions—and had run Vancouver of the Western Hockey League. He knew what it was to start up a new league and to be a rival of an established league. His football teams had bid against the National Football League for college talent.

Strangely, the Jets, despite the best record in the Western Division, only averaged about 6,300 fans a game at home.

"We filled every rink in the league except our own," says Stukus, who chalks it up to the fact that people

in Winnipeg had been accustomed to seeing top-level
hockey for years. They had been hosts to many international games.

The club had hoped that Hull's presence would
guarantee a turnout. Hatskin, the owner, had figured
that 1,000 seats a game would go to pay Hull's salary.
Fans were needed. Billboards proclaimed the "Hottest
Thing on Ice" was coming to town. In one 120-day
stretch, Stukus appeared at seventy-four luncheons,
dinners, and breakfasts. Did these relatively poor turn-
outs discourage management? Not at all. Explains
Stukus: "Bobby made us major league. He would have
been cheap for $5 million. Or $10 million. We got a
bargain, I would say the biggest bargain in the history
of sports. It made all our claims valid, that when we
told people and players they would be coming to a
major league—they believed us."

Ultimately, the league's first-year success—that it
was able to get off the ground at all—is laid to the fact
that the big stars did jump. "We had one thing going
for us," Stukus told one of his players. "And that was
the arrogance of the NHL. They never thought we'd do
it. But arrogance beat the Roman Empire—which was
damn near as powerful as the NHL."

The wooing of would-be jumpers reached its height
with the New York Raiders, originally headed by two
hockey fanatics. Players were brought into New York
and the merits of Fun City were extolled by the bosses—
Dick Wood and Sy Siegel. If it was entertainment the
player wanted then Marvin Milkes, the general manager, or Herb Elk, his assistant, or Camille Henry, the
coach, would take the prospects to dinner and Broadway
shows.

Henry recalls that "we tried to show them that New York was the place to be. You get exposed here as opposed to Ottawa or Quebec City." The exposures included dinner at the Playboy Club.

Yet, the Raiders had more problems than any other WHA team. Milkes tried. He was a baseball man (remember him refusing to pay for Jim Bouton's Gatorade in "Ball Four"?) turned hockey executive and often he would wind up deals at four or five o'clock in the morning. Elk stood at his right hand all the time. Elk was the only person in the organization, besides Henry, who could evaluate player talent. He had held a number of jobs as a publicity man in the minor leagues.

The Raiders set a record for reverse jumpers. Five players they signed—and made elaborate news conferences for—jumped back to the Establishment. They included Cowboy Bill Flett of the Flyers and Mike Robitaille of the Buffalo Sabres.

Still, the Raiders had high hopes. They would be playing in the world's most famous arena, Madison Square Garden, whose officials had estimated that between 4,000 to 6,000 season's tickets could be sold. But everyone overlooked the fact that the NHL had added a team to the New York area—the Islanders—and the NHL entrant quickly hurt the Raiders' chances by selling almost 8,000 season's seats. The Raiders just about managed to sell 2,000. That was hardly enough when they realized it would cost them almost $20,000 just to play a game in the Garden.

There were a couple of names on the squad, including Bobby Sheehan, New England-born, who had played hockey as a youngster under different pseudonyms. A natural ringer. Then there was Norm Ferguson, another who had done well in the NHL. The crop included, too, Ron Ward—who had scored the fewest points of any player in at least seventy games the season before. And there was Kent Douglas, once the rookie-of-the-year.

Another former rookie-of-the-year, Henry, was their leader. He looked different from his playing days. It was his toupee—given to him by Doug Mohns, a baldie from Chicago who had become a wig salesman. Henry was an honest man—if the situation were crazy, he'd say so. If he didn't like a player's attitude, he'd admit that, too, before the press. He attempted to whip his players into shape in a place called Bricktown, on the New Jersey shore. The nearest rink to theirs was fifty miles away. Henry didn't know all the players—in fact, he hardly knew any, since the regulars couldn't report right away. He had the players wear pieces of numbered cardboard safety-pinned to their backs so he could tell who was who.

In the first week of play Ward surpassed his scoring total for the previous year. But there were some tubby defensemen, whom Henry referred to as "overweight rhinoceroses." If a player were a light scorer, Henry said of him, "He couldn't hit the water if he fell out of a canoe."

Within a few weeks Milkes left, claiming "I've done the job I was brought in to do—get a hockey team started." Then the owners left the club. They turned it over to the league—or rather, the league took it off their hands. The payroll, the Garden rental, the travel expenses, the disappointingly low crowds—all conspired to make the prospects of losing a million dollars a bit frightening. A league administrator, James Browitt, was dispatched to run the team. Then Elk left. Henry remained. His trainer, Fraser Gleeson, became the traveling secretary while continuing to double as trainer. Henry and Gleeson disbursed meal money, made travel arrangements, and paid the hotels.

Meanwhile, there were no scouts. None had ever been hired. Henry ran things as best he could, but spent a good deal of his time assuring the players they would get paid. The Garden had been talked into lowering its rental, but money remained tight. Every few days there was a new rumor: the club would fold; it was being bought; it was being sold; it was being moved; it was getting a new general manager.

The team did get another administrator. John Coburn, one of the Whalers' founders, replaced Browitt, who went back to being a WHA executive. The team was a strange mixture on the ice, led by Ward, of all people. He was to turn in a 100-point season and had the distinction of being the league's first player to reach the fifty-goal and 100-point plateau. Sheehan, a lightning-quick forward with a mane of hair that would have helped him land the lead in a Passion Play, was an exciting performer. Ferguson was solid. Douglas was overweight.

Henry, with a bemused attitude toward his club, was less than stringent on workouts, although he kept fining all his overweight players. Then the club suffered assorted injuries, a situation that peaked in a game against Alberta. At the end of the contest the Raiders had six players on the ice and six on the bench. Small wonder, then, that the Oilers' Jim Harrison set a professional hockey record of ten points, on three goals and seven assists, in the game. The next day eight Raiders were admitted to hospitals.

The club's attendance started to pick up at the Garden after the first of the year, though. It wound up with the best second-half attendance of about 8,000 a game. The team was hoping to make the playoffs, although it was yielding goals at an alarming rate. It was scoring a lot—but most of the time it wasn't enough to compensate for the goals-against. The Raiders became the first team to give and get more than 300 goals in a season. Still, going into the final weeks it had a chance at the playoffs. The trouble was the Garden was booked with the circus. The Nassau Coliseum in Long Island was available, since the Islanders weren't about to make the NHL playoffs. Nassau County officials, after consulting with the Islanders, refused to give the Raiders the building. The Islanders had been unhappy with the Raiders—especially since two of their expansion draft picks, Ferguson and Garry Peters, had been lifted by their big-city rivals.

"What's good for the Islanders is good for Nassau County," said a Coliseum official in a latter-day rewording of the famous General Motors reference. Under threat of a lawsuit, however, the county gave in. But the Raiders failed to make the playoffs.

Ferguson was affected greatly by the whole affair. The Islanders had tried to get an injunction against him to stop him from performing for the Raiders. One night he and Henry left Ottawa. They had a court appearance in Brooklyn at noon the following day. The pair spent the night in Montreal, grabbed an early-morning flight to New York, and made the hearing. Ferguson brooded about it and didn't sleep after it was over. A day later, before a game, the team physician saw Henry and told him, "I'm going to send Fergy home right away. He's shaking." Soon, the injunction became academic. Within a few days Ferguson broke his leg and was lost for the season.

The great Maurice (Rocket) Richard, the man whose intense eyes gave the appearance of torches illuminating two caves on the side of a mountain, was the hero figure the Quebec Nordiques were going to build their team around.

Quebec was still another WHA city suffering from the second-city syndrome. Montreal was always first in La Belle Province. It didn't even pay for a potential group of people from Quebec to apply for entrance to the NHL. Montreal certainly would have refused. Anyway, the Coliseum wasn't big-league enough and the people in Quebec, many of them civil servants, couldn't pay big-league prices.

These were the knocks against a major league team in the big old city. But the proverbial "group of businessmen" was more optimistic. And their hopes ran highest after they signed Richard.

The Rocket was a brooding presence, the greatest goal-scorer of his time whose 544 career goals stood for a long time as the record. Even more, he was history's finest clutch scorer, the kind of man who sensed his greatness. Everyone in Montreal can tell stories of the time the Rocket returned from a broken leg and scored two goals to win, or he was knocked unconscious but returned dramatically in the final seconds to zero in on a goalie and, with players draped over him, shot the puck home to triumph.

In the playoffs, though, the Rocket was in a class by himself. His eighty-two goals were more than anyone else's. His eighteen game-winning goals stood alone and his overtime goals were twice as much as any other player had amassed. His regular season average of .556 goals a game—better than any modern player—soared to an average of .616 in Stanley Cup play. No one comes close.

When his days with the Canadiens were over, he joined the front office. His moods and his temper gradually caused a rift, though, and finally he left the club. He went into the fishing tackle business, operating out of his basement. When the Nordiques called, he saw a chance to get back at the Canadiens, an organization he had come to hate.

When the Nordiques signed him, it was generally expected that he would account for 5,000 season tickets sales—half the Coliseum's capacity. Now the Rocket was back, the years of brooding over. He had always been distressed that he had been overlooked when coaches were chosen for other clubs in the NHL. He always believed he had something to give to hockey, and now he was going to get his chance. Although the Canadiens and the Rocket hadn't been on speaking terms, he still received season tickets to the Montreal Forum. When he took the job with the Nordiques, his name was removed from the ticket list.

What did that matter? He was beginning a new life. The Nordiques' first player was the renowned J. C. Tremblay, the Canadiens' all-star defenseman. Tremblay was a fine player to begin a team with. He, too, had been unhappy in Montreal. The fickle fans often booed him for protracted stretches, then would turn around and shower him with praise. Jean-Claude was the prototype Montreal player. He performed with a Gallic flair, almost a sense of humor in the way he handled his stick like a baton. He would show the puck to an opponent and suddenly the puck would be gone—slid between the opponent's legs and J. C. would move around him and pick up his own pass.

But after getting Tremblay to jump, the Nordiques couldn't land much else in the way of talent. They went for French-Canadian players and signed practically anyone who could speak the language. The signing was done by Marius Fortier, a vice president. The owners had tried to hire a general manager, but by August—only a few weeks before training camp—still didn't have one. So Fortier, whose previous experience had been with the Quebec Remperts, a junior team, was pressed into service. In late August the club still was searching for players and he signed half a dozen of them two weeks before camp opened. Fortier didn't know professional contracts and clauses. He never had to pay his amateur juniors quite so much money as the players were asking now. Yet, he was in charge of a payroll worth more than $500,000.

To compound the difficulties, Richard wasn't around. As part of his deal on signing, the Nordiques had permitted him to skip training camp so he could go to the Team Canada-Russia matches—in Canada and the Soviet Union—on private business. Thus, Richard wasn't even at his team's camp opening. Maurice Filion took his place. When Richard finally joined his club— which was paying him more money than he had ever earned as a player—it was only ten days to the start of the season. He knew no players on the club except Tremblay. This was an unheard-of situation. But if management hadn't been in awe of Richard they never would have permitted it. And if Richard hadn't been Richard, he wouldn't have dared ask for it. A coach, after all, is supposed to coach—especially a coach who had never seen the players, and was attempting to mold a club of strangers into a unit.

Finally, the season started. The Nordiques helped unveil the WHA with a game at Cleveland. This was what the Rocket had been prepared for—all those years under pressure, having to make the right decisions in front of thousands of people. He had shone under pressure, hadn't he? The Nordiques lost, 2-0. And Richard wanted to quit.

He complained that he didn't know the game after twelve years, that the players had changed, that he didn't know if he could make the right moves, that there was too much pressure. Fortier convinced him to come back to Quebec for the Nordiques' first home game. Rocket agreed. Two days later he returned to Quebec, and the Nordiques shut out Alberta. They had won, and the pressure was off. Or was it? Richard quit—this time for good.

"He couldn't stand the pressure any more," said a club official. "He just seemed a little bit mixed up, and his heart wasn't in it. It was funny. He wanted his chance to prove he could coach. He got his chance, and then he never proved anything. He was traumatized."

Filion replaced Richard for good behind the bench. Tremblay went on to produce under pressure in a season that would see only one player on the team play every game. The injuries and the inexpert defense put burdens on Tremblay. In one game that went overtime, he saw action for sixty-three minutes. He averaged close to forty minutes a game in playing time. And he wound up with eighty-nine points—the only defenseman in modern big-league history, except for Bobby Orr, to lead his team in scoring.

Presumably, the Rocket meanwhile was working on getting his season's tickets back from the Canadiens.

Nick Mileti, a flamboyant Cleveland lawyer, tried to break into the WHA by buying the heart of the New York Rangers. He offered million-dollar deals to Rod Gilbert, Brad Park, and Vic Hadfield—and helped to make them rich when they used the offers as a wedge to remain in New York.

Mileti collected athletes the way some people collect bubble gum cards. He owned the Cleveland Indians baseball team, the Cleveland Cavaliers of the American Basketball Association, the Cleveland Barons of the American Hockey League and, for good measure, the Cleveland Arena.

He really wanted a National Hockey League team.

He made his pitch to the league when it was accepting applications for two more franchises. He rented a suite and built a scale model of a proposed new 17,000-seat arena. The model cost over $10,000. Then he filled the room with whiskey and snacks and invited everyone to see his grand plans. People were impressed and he was a front-runner to get a franchise for the 1974–75 season. But while the league owners were deliberating, they received a telegram from a United States Senator asking that a franchise be considered for Washington, D.C. That was like a sergeant asking a private to "volunteer." You volunteer. The NHL was already distressed by Federal investigations into its structure, as well as a host of lawsuits that alleged anti-trust violations. So Washington was granted a franchise.

That still left Mileti with a good shot at the big time. His stiffest opposition was supposed to come from Kansas City. He didn't think they'd be much trouble. Later, some of Mileti's associates were to charge that the man who was to put up the Kansas City arena, if a franchise were awarded there, was the same man who was asked to pass on the merits of other applicants. Cleveland believed it was playing with a stacked deck. After all, they said, if you're going to be given a multi-million-dollar construction job, would you turn it down by saying the building should be put up in another city? So Washington along with Kansas City, was granted a franchise. Exit Nick Mileti from the NHL.

Two weeks later he was in the WHA. It was late June, and the season would start in a few months. Mileti had to work fast.

First came his offers to the Rangers. Then he spoke to Cheevers. Mileti was handling his own negotiations. He didn't have an organization, but he was well versed in contracts. He landed Cheevers, and it took $200,000 a year for seven years.

In Cheevers he had, perhaps, the calmest goalie in hockey. If he was fazed, he never showed it. He had the reputation as one of the best clutch goalies around, although his average had never been much to show off about. Cheevers was, all in all, an excellent choice for a club that was starting from scratch. His style would also keep his teammates calm. If the goalie is confident, then the teammates are, too. Cheevers was the man who once had been in the nets while the Bruins lost by 10-2 to the Black Hawks. When the game was over Emms stormed into the room.

"What the hell happened out there?" Emms demanded.

"Simple," Cheevers replied. "Roses are red, violets are blue, they got 10, we only got two."

Mileti also hired Chuck Catto as his assistant general manager. Catto had been the player personnel director for the Golden Seals of the NHL. Within a few weeks Catto got three Seals to jump to the Cleveland Crusaders.

Fred Glover, dismissed as Seals' coach a year before, also was hired to help lure more players to Cleveland. Glover didn't stay long.

"I was on a three-week vacation," relates one of the Crusaders' front-office people. "Glover was hired while I was away. By the time I came back he was gone."

Glover was rehired by the Seals' boss, Finley. He returned to the Seals as executive vice president, a job that had been held by four different people in two seasons under Finley.

Despite Mileti's persuasiveness in signing players, he couldn't find anyone to coach the club. When training camp opened in September at Bowling Green University, no one was behind the bench. Bill Needham, a scout, was told to direct the players until a coach had been found. Six days before the season was to open there still was no coach. Needham was signed.

He did a good job, planning his style around Cheevers. It was a defensively oriented squad and Cheevers was the leader. The goalie kept his club loose on long plane trips by playing trivia games. Before long, everyone knew that Elmo Lincoln played the first movie Tarzan. Cheevers's roommate was the number two goalie, Bob Whidden, who claimed "that Gerry has made me so smart. I've got to read the papers every day so he doesn't stump me."

It hadn't snowed in thirteen years in Houston—until the Aeros came to town. As if to greet the WHA, which was bringing big-league hockey to Texas for the first time, it snowed three times.

The only thing the Aeros would have appeared to have in common with Houston was the nickname—a spiritual descendant of the Astros. The club wasn't even originally Texan—it had been shifted from Dayton, where a proposed arena wasn't going to be built.

Some of the club's owners were confident Houston could support big-league hockey, although it had never shown much willingness to turn out for the minor league brand. A study undertaken by the owners of prime market areas in the United States showed that Houston was ready for hockey.

Sam Houston must have turned over in his grave when this foreign sport was brought into the arena named for him. Not many fans turned out, but they were noisy. They were, after all, Texans. Some people say the crowds in the Sam Houston Coliseum were the noisiest and most enthusiastic in hockey.

Houstonites had to be convinced. Management attended dozens of civic dinners. And every place they went they brought along hundreds of tickets. What did it matter how many people got in for free—just so long as they could see hockey. Maybe the next time they'd come and pay their way.

To help the fans learn something about the game the club's radio announcer, Jerry Trupiano, mixed anecdotes and play-by-play along with pointers. But to bolster the ratings, the team hired a former football trainer, Bobby Brown, to provide the "color" on the home broadcasts.

Brown was a Houston celebrity, who had once been named the National Football League's trainer of the year. He was in demand as an after-dinner speaker and people in Houston knew his name. It didn't matter much that his knowledge of hockey was somewhat limited.

There was one game in which the Aeros were being bombed in the first period by the Nordiques.

Trupiano, in the best traditions of objective broadcasting, said to Brown, "Bobby, the Aeros aren't going too well."

Brown replied: "Well, the reason is they just can't get their wide-open conservative style untracked tonight."

As time went by, though, whatever their style was finally untracked itself. They began to win around Christmas-time and began a mini-tradition of taking clutch games. One time they were trailing by 2-1 with a few minutes to play. They tied it and won in overtime. A few days later they trailed by 4-1 in the final period and won, 5-4. In this respect they were similar to another first-year team, the St. Louis Blues, who also began to win at midseason when they joined the NHL. There was even an ex-Blue in the front office, Doug Harvey. He was named assistant coach to Bill Dineen, following many years of brooding about his fate. A great defenseman, Harvey had been shunned by the Establishment and often complained that "there must be room in hockey for a guy that was an all-star defenseman." He finally got his chance again in Houston.

The club's clown was Cleland Lindsay (Keke) Mortson, who once amused his teammates on a long flight to Edmonton by standing in front of the plane and announcing: "I have good news and bad news. First the good news. We're going to land. The bads news is that's because we're out of gasoline."

Traveling proved burdensome for the Aeros, whose closest rival was in Chicago, 900 miles away. They had their share of problems on the road, including an eighteen-day road trip, and the night in Boston their bus driver left the hotel for the arena. Twenty minutes later the driver returned to the hotel, unable to find his way.

Then there was the game in St. Paul. The players had warmed up and were ready for the battle. But no referee. They skated and skated, and shot pucks at the goalie and the fans got restless. Then someone decided to look for referee Ray Thomas. He had been locked in his dressing room.

By the time the Chicago Cougars took the ice they had three different sets of owners. When the final (perhaps) bosses, the Kaiser brothers, bought the club they assumed they were getting title to it free and clear. They quickly were hit by a lawsuit from one of the previous owners, who claimed the team still was his.

The constant, the man who was supposed to make things go, was Ed Short. His hockey background was nonexistent, yet he was the carry-over general manager when the Kaisers took control. Short had been a baseball man most of his life, as road secretary, publicist, and general manager of the Chicago White Sox.

By August, a few weeks before camp, he had signed one player—Bob Kelly of the Flyers. Kelly jumped back when his money never appeared. So with training camp just around the corner, the Cougars didn't have one player under contract.

It was typical of some of the anomalies of a first-year league that Short and another former baseball g.m., Milkes of the Raiders, often talked potential trades once the season finally began.

"Here we are, two old baseball men who know nothing about hockey, and we're each extolling our players," said Milkes. "It's a funny situation."

Short remained on the job because he still was under contract and the new owners didn't know what else to do. They had only days to prepare, and figured they might as well go with what they had. By the time camp started Short had signed bodies—only one of them, Rosaire Paiement, had played a full campaign in the NHL the season before. Only two other players, Rod Zaine and Larry Mavety, had even been in the big leagues the previous season.

There was one saver, though: Reggie Fleming. He was one of the most popular players ever to appear with the Black Hawks, and he was available. He had played with Salt Lake City of the Western League following a long major-league career that had included four seasons with the Hawks.

Reggie was an honest player who had no illusions about his talent or the role he was always called on to play. He was supposed to be a shaker, a guy who offered himself in fights and would get penalized just to stir up things, or take a damaging opponent off the ice with him. He had never scored twenty goals in the big leagues. Indeed, until he got to Salt Lake he never even had twenty goals in seventeen professional seasons. He got his name in the record books twice—for leading the league in penalties one season, and for committing a record thirty-seven penalty minutes in a single game. Even that record was broken.

But Reggie had made his home in Chicago and sent his kids to school there. He had become a Chicago personality, appearing on talk shows, always ready to speak before youth groups.

The coach of the club was Marcel Pronovost, who had played in 1,206 NHL games—and only eleven other players had appeared in more. In fact, he saw more big-league action than all his players combined.

"Marcel doesn't know what quitting means," says a club official. Perhaps he learned—at least what losing was. By Christmas it was apparent the Cougars were on the way to gaining the distinction of amassing the WHA's worst record in its first year.

There were some pleasant surprises on the team, though. Jim McLeod was saved from the obscurity of minor-league goaltending and posted almost a .500 percentage. But the club's other goalie, Andre Gill, won only four of his twenty-eight decisions. Another minor-leaguer, Bobby Sicinski, became the team's leading point-getter and the International Amphitheatre fans had something to cheer about when Sicinski centered the grandly named Power Line.

In January Short was dismissed and one Jacques Demers, lately of the Chateaugay juniors near Montreal, took over Short's duties.

Losing made Pronovost unhappy. Defeat was simply something he couldn't accept. He refused to let his club play out the string, even though with ten games remaining his club was all but mathematically eliminated from the playoffs and was locked in last place. Oh, there was a chance to make the playoffs, all right. All the Cougars had to do was win their last ten games—while two of the clubs above them each lost their last ten—and Chicago would be in the playoffs.

Pronovost became highly insulted after one game when he was asked if he were planning for the following season already, since his chances at that point were virtually nil. He exploded and screamed, "Are you trying to tell me I don't have a chance? How could I tell my guys that?" Eventually, he had to.

The Minnesota Fighting Saints, led by a college-trained coach-general manager, slowed the importation of hockey players into the United States by putting nine Americans on the club. The last time that had been tried was more than thirty years before, when the Black Hawks attempted to bolster attendance and iced an all-American team.

Glen Sonmor, the man who led the Saints, didn't do things quite the orthodox way. He is a former forward-defenseman who had two brief flings with the New York Rangers during the mid-1950s. His career was cut short when he was injured during a minor league game and wound up losing an eye. Instead of pouting, he went back to college, acquired two degrees, and went into college coaching, first at Ohio State and then the University of Minnesota.

Of course, the pros were a revelation. He was selected for the dual roles by the usual conglomerate of businessmen who wanted a hockey franchise. A new arena, the St. Paul Civic Center, was due to open in mid-season and why waste a brand new building? Sonmor soon discovered that "when you talk contracts you don't talk to players—just their lawyers and agents."

It bothered him that most of the players he signed were locked into no-cut, no-trade deals. Perhaps, he hoped, their pride would motivate them through the season. "Still," he admits, "it's not the sort of situation you like to get yourself into. You don't have anything to hold over their heads."

Sonmor also learned about "babysitting"—the process of covering up an athlete so that no one else can approach him. "I used to hear about babysitting while I was in college. You know, one team would send over a scout or coach and keep the kid unavailable so another coach wouldn't be able to get near him. But I never experienced it until I came here—and did it myself."

Sonmor babysat for Billy Klatt, a Minneapolis-born

youngster who had scored thirty-four goals with the Bruins' top farm club. He knew that Milt Schmidt, the Bruins' g.m., was after Klatt, and after him hard. Sonmor had to get young Klatt away from Schmidt's clutches. First, the Saints flew Klatt and Sonmor to the Tom Webster golf tournament in Niagara Falls ("That was funny, most guys don't have golf tourneys named after them till they're dead," says Sonmor). He took Klatt there deliberately. He knew Webster would be there, and so would Rick Ley and Brad Selwood—all NHL players who were going to jump.

"I wanted Billy in the sort of atmosphere that was conducive to jumping," explains Sonmor.

At the height of this conduciveness, Sonmor convinced Klatt to call Schmidt and tell him that he had decided to go with the Fighting Saints. Sonmor stood at his side while Klatt made the call.

"Then I jumped on a plane with Billy and we flew back to St. Paul to hold a press conference before Boston could come back and make him another offer."

Sonmor picked up a bunch of other American-born boys, most of whom had played in college. At one time, the American collegian was scoffed at by pro hockey experts. People asked Sonmor, "Where the hell did these guys ever play?" But Sonmor knew that American collegians were pretty good. They had, after all, finished second in the Olympics to the Russians.

By the time training camp rolled around Sonmor's selections didn't look quite so bad. The Russians had given a hockey lesson to the NHL's best and now North American hockey was re-evaluating itself. Perhaps it had something to learn from the Russians after all. That didn't surprise Sonmor. "I knew my guys had played against good calibre hockey in the past. But when they played the Russians, people didn't think much of them

and anyone the Russians beat, therefore, weren't supposed to be that good."

Because Sonmor wanted a college-style team—one
that could skate like the wind and move the puck around
—he wound up with a bunch of little guys. "I learned that
we lacked size," Sonmor admits. As the season wore
along his smallish players were knocked around quite a
bit. They easily got tired. Everyone ran at them.

The players weren't afraid of fans, though. After a
game at Ottawa some fanatics were jeering the Saints
as they filed into the dressing room. Then one of them
reached toward the bench and grabbed Sonmor's velvet
jacket and said, "Yoo hoo, Liberace!" The players still in
the runway saw the fan's hands on their coach and they
leaped in. Meanwhile, half a dozen Saints were in the
dressing room, unaware of what was going on. They
started to take off their shirts when someone asked,
"Hey, where's everybody else?" They ran outside, saw
the brawl, and mixed in. Some of the fighters were bare-
chested and Sonmor looked at the scene and said to himself, "This must really be something. They ripped our
guys' shirts off."

Later, one of the players told Sonmor, "Those fans
can call us anything they want. But when they called
you Liberace, it was just too much."

Ottawa never forgave the Nationals for trying to get
into two other cities first. By the time their first season
ended Ottawa attempted to apologize, but the Nationals
wouldn't accept—and moved elsewhere.

The Nationals were one of the original $25,000 bar-
gain franchises in the new league. The trouble was they
couldn't find a place to play. Toronto, of course, was the
natural base for a club from Ontario. But Maple Leaf
Gardens wanted a guarantee of more than $25,000 a

game. That was a bit much for the owner, Doug Michel, who made his money as an electrical contractor and wasn't about to blow it. Then the club tried Hamilton, the big mining city not far away. Hamilton's mayor wanted more than Michel was willing to pay.

That left Ottawa, the nation's capital.

It is one of the more tradition-bound cities in Canada, as well as one that gets along on a fixed income. So when the people first heard of the WHA they treated it, for the most part, as some sort of joke. However, when it came to paying for the Civic Center, there was more realism.

The usual rental for the building was about $1,000 a game or 15 percent of the gate, whichever was greater. The junior team, the Ottawa 67s, didn't have to guarantee the Center management a dime. But the Nationals had to guarantee $100,000 over the course of the first season.

Michel quickly looked for more financing and got a Buffalo businessman, Nick Trbovich, to back him.

In order to meet the guarantee under normal circumstances the Nationals would have to average 5,500 fans a game. They averaged 2,900. Because of the low price scale, the average gross was about $10,000. Multiply that by 39 home games and it meant that more than one-fourth of their gross income had to go for rental. That was just about double what other events in the building had to pay.

Ottawans were extremely money conscious. They could see their 67s, who had the most highly acclaimed junior in hockey in Denis Potvin, for $1 or $2. Although the top price for the Nationals was only $6.50, these seats went begging.

"What happened," explains one club official, "was the people would buy the Nats' $3.50 and $4.50 seats.

But when those seats were gone, instead of buying the $5.50 or $6.50 seats they'd just turn around and go home."

Promotions were attempted. "All they did was lower our prices and not bring in any more fans," moaned the ticket manager. The club, for example, tried a student half-price policy. But students would go on line, get their tickets, and then pass their I.D. cards to people behind them—often getting six or seven half-price seats.

The stick-night promotion was a little more successful. About 5,000 people turned out, and children were to get their sticks when the game was over. After all, no one wants a few thousand people holding sticks at a hockey game.

As luck would have it, the game was tied after the third period. Some fans forgot that the WHA has a sudden-death overtime period. They went to get their sticks, got them, and then were told the game was still on. So they returned to their seats. When the thousands of other fans saw some carrying sticks, they immediately left to get their sticks. By the time the overtime started about 4,000 youngsters were in their seats waving sticks —a situation management feared. Luckily, the game wound up tied. No one used his stick for anything nasty.

For most of the season the Nats' sticks were as about as effective on the ice. The club rutted around last place in the Eastern Division. Then it started to make its move. It won eleven of twelve games and became a play-off contender. But another $100,000 was due the arena for the following season. It had to be put up by March 15. The city had taken over the building. The Nats wanted to renegotiate the deal, but one of the Ottawa aldermen said: Pay or we lock the doors. The club immediately looked for another place to play.

They found one—Maple Leaf Gardens. Just a few

months before the Gardens had asked prohibitive rents. But the Maple Leaf hockey team again had failed to make the NHL playoffs, and there would be an idle building around. The Gardens cut its rental by two-thirds—and the Nationals accepted. They would play their playoff games in the Gardens. The club made the playoffs. Even though Ottawa now had changed its mind and wanted the Nationals back, the club moved into the Gardens for the playoffs. They drew 9,000 people in the two games and grossed about $50,000—more than 10 percent of what they had taken in for thirty-nine games in Ottawa.

The Nats were so stunned that they decided to move the club to Toronto and rename them the Toros. But first, there was a playoff against the New England Whalers. The Whalers won. But one of the last acts committed by an Ottawa National player typified the struggles of the season. The club had just lost to the Whalers and was to leave in the morning for Ottawa.

One of the players stayed out rather late—in fact, he came home in the morning, just when the team bus was ready to go to the airport. When he arrived at the hotel to get his belongings he discovered the elevators weren't working. He walked up twenty-three flights to his room, packed, and came down twenty-three flights. He got on the team bus. Then he realized he forgot his plane ticket. He walked up the twenty-three flights, retrieved it, and came down again. Ninety-two flights of stairs. Perhaps the elevator service is better in Toronto.

Eight

"YOU'RE AN ASSHOLE for jumping back," Bobby Orr greeted Derek. "I wanted to tell you that first before somebody asked me."

Derek's return to the Bruins wasn't quite ruffles and flourishes. The Stanley Cup champagne had gone stale. Before he stepped foot in the locker room, Orr collared him. Orr had always had a special way with Derek, and Derek respected him.

"Bobby's the kind of guy who always took everything personally. It gets to him," explains Derek. "Maybe that's why he has upset stomachs all the time. If a player's got a problem, Bobby tries to solve it—family problem, playing, home life, anything. If a guy's in a car accident, Bobby's there to bail him out. He works twenty-four hours a day keeping everybody healthy and happy. If we're not playing well, Bobby's the first guy to blame himself. He does so many good things for people, things they're not even aware of because he doesn't want them to know. And then he gets rapped in the press for being uncommunicative and it bothers him. He'd be a lot better off if he just paid attention to himself."

When Orr spoke, Derek listened. And Orr proceeded to give Derek a lecture:

"Turk, you were wrong to jump back. You had a moral obligation to remain. I'm happy to have you back, happy that you're with the club. I think you can really help us, but personally I think you hurt yourself and you should have stayed in Philadelphia and fought it out. You committed yourself to a contract, you signed it, you should have honored it. Sure, when you jumped you hurt us—you hurt me. But a contract's a contract."

Orr concluded his speech: "You've got to be very strong now. It's going to be hard, because you've got to be humble. Work hard, and don't throw the money in the guys' faces. Some of the guys are awful upset about you coming back. They're wondering how you're going to act. They're just looking for an excuse to nail you."

Two days after Derek agreed to rejoin the Bruins, Sinden dismissed Johnson as coach and replaced him with Guidolin, a former zoot-suiter who twirled a key chain and wore wing-tipped shoes when, as a sixteen-year-old during World War II, he became the youngest player ever to appear in the NHL. Two days after Guidolin was named coach, the Bruins officially announced that Derek was back.

There was much that was similar between the pair. When they were younger they were known as the local "hard guys," tough-talking, wise-cracking, leather-jacketed. In the 1940s Guidolin had a thick head of hair that had earned him the nickname "Buffalo head." They even had similar playing styles.

"I was a tough, rough guy. I wasn't afraid," relates

Guidolin. "I was a hungry guy who came from a poor family and I needed the money. To get me out of the NHL, guys would have to fight me out. I had a reputation as a hard-nosed hockey player." But Guidolin realized now that he was "on the other side of the fence. I realized the mistakes I had made with my mouth. I didn't always say the proper things about management. They're up against different pressures, too. The way I feel now, management was doing things the proper way, always for the benefit of the players. The players now are getting enough money to produce. It's nice to get a big fat contract. It's nice to be a millionaire, but you got to produce."

So he told Derek, "You'll have to come back to our way of thinking. You'll have to work yourself into shape. You'll kill penalties and you'll sit on the bench the rest of the time. You'll do what you're told."

Guidolin immediately shaped up his club. Their tongues were hanging out after the first practice. He didn't believe in off-days and he certainly didn't believe in not giving the proverbial "110 percent." The Bruins were going to stop their country-club living and were going to be whipped into a fighting machine again.

He was leading a collection of players who were each making more money than he had dreamed of when he was a player, when he had fought for players' rights and screamed in the dressing room against the excesses of management. Guidolin remembers himself as "kind of a rebel when it came to the dressing room. I was always in the front leading something. That's how we started to get this pension. We were rebels. The only thing is we're not benefiting from it. The kids are—but it was our hard work that got them all this."

They were going to work for their money, for the pension that would enable each player on the ice to get

$1,000 a year for each year he played in the National Hockey League. Guidolin wouldn't see any of that pension money, and it bothered him that $30,000-a-year hockey players were receiving $100,000, "just because they got you by the neck and threaten to jump to the other league."

Oh, it was different all right when he was playing. In those days if you didn't produce you didn't get paid. There were no long-term deals that guaranteed you $100,000 next year even if you scored only fifteen goals this year. And there were outside interests, so much for the players to do. Why, they weren't devoting their lives to the game of hockey—not the way they used to.

Yet, Guidolin respected Derek. He knew he had always been a hungry player, the type they would have to try to beat up to get out of the game. And no one quite was able to do that. Guidolin hoped that Derek simply would quit "commentating" on management, keep his mouth shut, work himself into condition, and do his job. He believed he knew how to handle Derek. He was the kind of player who wanted to play, he wanted ice time. He would have to learn to be patient, that he wasn't going to step in as the third-line center, a job being handled by a rookie named Greg Sheppard. If Derek was going to mouth off, Guidolin figured he knew how to handle that, too. "He's the kind of guy who likes to say things on the spur of the moment. You've just got to give it right back to him," says Guidolin.

A kid named Fred O'Donnell was wearing number 16, Derek's old number. "Can I get it back?" he asked Sinden. "No way," was the answer. O'Donnell also was sitting in Derek's old spot in the Bruins' dressing room, two spots in from the door, right next to Esposito. "What about my old locker?" "Ask the trainer," was the answer.

Derek returned to the dressing room for the first time in nine months. "It was no big deal. I just walked right in, put on my equipment, and went right out to practice. Oh, some of the guys laughed when I put on number 27."

He had asked the assistant trainer, Frosty Forristall, for his old spot back. Forristall asked O'Donnell, who wanted to keep it. Then he asked O'Donnell if he could get number 16 again.

"Sure," replied O'Donnell. "For two thousand bucks."

Derek trudged out to the rink. The players started to applaud him, tapping their sticks on the ice in the traditional hockey cheer.

"Hey, Moses has returned," shouted one.

"It's baby Jesus and he's going to save us," called out another.

But the feeling came back for Derek, a nostalgic sort of glow. And he was grateful especially to Orr and Esposito who, he was to say later, "paved the way for me." Orr, he had known, "was always good. But I never realized how fine he was. And Espie, he's always been proud of his situation, how well he's done in life, and he doesn't have any hang-ups. And Eddie Johnston greeted me warmly. But Don Awrey got vicious."

"Hey Turk, what do you care if you make a bad pass—you've got enough bread," said Awrey.

"Look," Orr told Awrey, "I don't mind you knocking. It's fun to knock. But you're getting vicious, you're cutting deep. So let's everybody relax."

In the back of Derek's mind was this: I don't mind eating humble pie. But I don't want it shoved down my throat. I'm here because I want to be. I didn't come back here and tell the guys I'm in Boston for a lot less than other NHL teams were offering me. I'm costing myself $100,000 just to play for the Bruins.

"But I took it," says Derek. "And I realized that getting the money gave me all the confidence I would ever need. I wasn't afraid to get upset any more."

Esposito has always had a special fondness for Derek. Or perhaps it is simply bemusement.

"God bless Derek," says Esposito, a bear of a man, with a slouching posture and an amiable disposition. "I never would say anything to him about the jumping or the money. Who's to say that what a guy does with his life is right or wrong? From the time he first left I wished him well. Oh, I was hurt. Sure. What bothered me was the club was being broken up. It was a winning team, a team of eighteen, nineteen, twenty guys. Each of those guys had a role to play, and Derek had a big part. I suppose my feelings were mixed. On the one hand I felt happy for him and his big offer. On the other hand, I was sorry to see him go."

In some ways Esposito is the most realistic of the Bruins. He likes to say, "Hockey became a job for me the first day I got paid to skate." Yes, he enjoys it, but he also knows it's a living—and money has always been very important to Espie. Money and integrity. He's got a fetish about making sure that the hockey products that have his name on them are as good as can be. He's even sent personal replies to a child who bought a Phil Esposito street hockey puck and found a flaw in it. Like Derek, Esposito also had his own business adviser, a Harvard man named Fred Sharf whose aim in life was to see that when Phil Esposito was thirty-five, he didn't have to worry about playing hockey again. Esposito had learned that he had to take care of himself. He, too, had found himself laboring under a multi-year contract when he broke into the NHL and, in his first full season, scored more than twenty goals but was stuck with virtually the same money for the second season. Certainly, Esposito wasn't going to rap a fellow player who had tried to get the best deal he could.

"I remember that a couple of guys were wondering if Derek could come back," says Esposito. "They thought that he must be crazy thinking he could make it again after all that happened to him. But I knew Derek pretty good, and I knew that there was no way he'd be content to sit on the bench. He'd force himself into shape. I told Derek that if he came back to us, he had to quit scurrying around on the outside, that we needed him to play hockey. I told him that if he wasn't in shape to forget it —that we needed immediate help."

"Well, Phil, I'll just be killing penalties for a while," Sanderson told him.

"If I'm out there and you get tired and you need me to forecheck for you, just let me know," Esposito advised him.

All in all, Esposito was "glad to have him back. He's good. He's funny."

Sinden was watching Derek's return very carefully and closely. He was looking for signs. "I wanted to see that his behavior on the ice was such that he wasn't going to excommunicate himself from his teammates by taking silly misconducts or getting angry if he didn't play enough. I knew it was difficult enough, him being a regular player over the years, to have to sit there. I wondered how he was going to take all this. He had been quite a player for me. You know all the lines he ever played on for the Bruins—he never was blessed with high-scoring, play-making wingers. He always had the checkers, the third-line wings, the Westfalls, the Don Marcottes."

The Bruins had changed. Derek had changed. It had only been nine months since the Stanley Cup, but it wasn't the same. "It wasn't the gung-ho, hitting club it used to be," Derek discovered. "It was mature, elegant— and it had lost its fun. But, hey, I'm twenty-six years old now, and not the kid I used to be either."

Under Guidolin, though, the club started to produce. It became a winner. Slowly, Derek got into shape and then one day he was in a game. He remembers that "they still loved me in Boston my first game back. I think I killed six penalties. But still, I felt like an outsider. I wasn't necessary. I wasn't needed. Bep had told me I wasn't going to take Sheppard's job. I was just going to be a fill-in, do the right thing, and then we'd see about next year."

He had hoped that he would get a month to prepare his return. But he was needed immediately. The Bruins had to turn things around, to get out of third place. His first game back had been on a Saturday afternoon against the Pittsburgh Penguins. "I wish it were the Rangers or the Canadiens," thought Derek.

The old man had told him at the hospital: "Derek, when you come back just play defensively. Don't get fancy until you get in shape." He put on the uniform with the number 27, the one that Forristall, the assistant trainer, had told him would make him a scorer. "It's Frank Mahovlich's number," said Forristall. "If Mahovlich can do it, you can do it."

As Derek dressed for his return, he suddenly found himself more nervous than he had ever been in his life. And for the first time he worried about giving the puck away or making a mistake. He had always been an intuitive player, one who didn't hedge, who grabbed the main chance when he could. Now he was thinking conservatively—would he lose the puck?

Around him his teammates went through their daily rituals. Esposito stuck his big right hand into the bubble gum box and snared twenty pieces. Always the same thing, the hand into the box before every game. Then he set them in a pile next to him on the bench. He unwrapped one, chewed it for a few seconds, taking most of the sugar. He spit it out into the pail and unwrapped another piece of gum. Derek wondered whether anyone would step on Phil's stick. That would drive the big man crazy. Derek had seen Espie slash at someone for doing that.

McKenzie wasn't around any more and so there was no one to mess with Esposito's head by crossing sticks in the locker room. Esposito simply couldn't abide crossed sticks and McKenzie took delight in torturing him.

Cheevers, the meticulous goalie, wasn't there either. He was constantly cutting and refitting his equipment, demanding more padding in the gloves, or less in the chest protector. He would insist on padding over a bone in his finger that Derek knew would never get hit if Cheevers played for thirty years. Cheevers also switched masks continuously.

Green also wasn't there. He was finicky, but had become obsessive after his head accident, forever trying on new helmets. The helmets took his mind off the other equipment—the gloves with the fingers an eighth of an inch too long, the shin pads that were too tight.

Walton, as usual, had what Derek called "a goddamned delicatessen." There were neatly stacked rolls of tape near Shakey. Six long strips of tape, each the exact same length, were stuck to the edge of the bench to use on his gear. There were three cups—including a beer-sized plastic one—filled with ice. One was for his Gatorade, one for water, and the beer cup to be filled with grape juice five minutes before the period was over. He liked his grape juice cold. No one ever touched his tape. That would drive Shakey up the wall, even if he was the only Bruin certified as sane.

Number 27. Yet, it had a certain ring of character to it. Not, perhaps, connoting the same puissance as a number under 10—say 9, which Rocket Richard, Gordie Howe, and Bobby Hull wore. Or even a 4, which Orr and Jean Beliveau carried. There was an easy identification with a one-digit number. Richard—9. That was it. No frills. Hull—9. You saw those low numbers and you made an instant connection. Yet, in his fashion, Derek had done the same with the innocuous 16. People had started to say, when someone on another club wore 16, "Oh, Derek Sanderson's number, isn't it?" He had taken the banal and lifted it, reshaped it.

One thing he knew he didn't want—22. That had been nothing but bad luck for him. He wore it in a junior B tryout and they had given him "two retarded wingers." He passed the puck to one, and the other wing slammed into him. Derek was out of action and blew the tryout. He switched numbers. Then when he made it to the junior A, they gave him 22 again. He had a bad season. He switched numbers. On his first day as a rookie, Forristall slipped him number 22. Derek, the rookie, told him, "No damn way I'm going to wear that number." Forristall told him, "What are you, a nut? You'll wear what we give you." Derek prevailed, and had worn the 16 since—until now.

But it was time to get dressed. Derek did the left

skate first. He always does when he wants to change his luck. If he scores in the first period he will leave his skates on through the intermission. But if he doesn't get a goal, he will take off his skates.

Orr was sitting next to Dallas Smith. He picked up his own stick and Smith's and started to walk around the room. Always with two sticks, that was how Derek had remembered Bobby. Then Orr went over to each player and touched him. That was for luck, and he did it every game. Eighteen touches. Of course, Orr was careful not to step on Espie's sticks, or to disturb the order of Esposito's gear. Esposito's stick was perfectly parallel to the bench. Esposito would square it off if it wasn't just right. Then the left hand glove was carefully laid to the left of the stick, palm up. The right hand glove was placed on the opposite end. The heels of both gloves were in perfect line with the bottom of the stick.

Derek didn't like to mess with other player's superstitions. "They might fool around with yours," he explains. He didn't remember where they had started. He knew his mother had a strange one that she had carried with her from Scotland. Each New Year's Eve, on the stroke of midnight, she'd leave through the back door and carry a lump of coal, a piece of wood, and a slice of bread. Then she'd come back around the house and walk in the front door. She had fuel, food, shelter. These are what they symbolized, that she was starting the New Year with the necessities of life. "She did that every year and I was never hungry a day in my life," says Derek. "Maybe there was something to it. Anyway, the way I see it—why tempt fate?"

Derek was ready to go. The skates had been sharpened like a knife. That was how he liked it, how he had always told the trainers he wanted his skates prepared.

He also liked them rockered. This way the blade made contact with the ice on only a very small surface, creating less friction. It permitted him to pivot easily, to play what he calls his "slippery-slidey game."

As he left the dressing room Walton stood at the door, touching each player as he left. Only one more ritual remained.

Derek had thought the crowd would be 50-50. Half for him, half against. But it sounded like 95-5 in his favor as he stepped onto the ice in the old arena, spotlighted under the dozens of naked hanging lights that were installed after color television came along.

He had been on that ice the last week or so, working out with the Boston Braves. His old friend, Matt Ravlich, had taken over the Braves' coaching after Guidolin was promoted to the Bruins. Derek had thrown up on that ice for the first time the past week, the nervousness of returning combined with the physical strain making his stomach a simmering volcano. Somehow he was ready for a game. Everyone had driven him. Even Ravlich, who had gone out drinking with him one night, only to find in the morning that he had become the Braves' coach and had to command Derek in the workouts.

Ravlich had once told his players: "The only way you get to the NHL is by hard work, isn't that right, Derek?" And then he sent Derek out on the ice, "back and forth twice." And Derek had thrown up twice while Ravlich and the players laughed.

But that was the way hockey players commiserated with one another, and Derek accepted it. He even laughed about it. Laughter—that was the thing that these professional athletes used when things got rough. At times, of course, their humor was almost sick. A year before there had been an extremely tough workout, and the guys came into the dressing room kicking at buckets and cursing their lot. McKenzie wasn't there. He had been excused because his brother had died. Ace Bailey fumed and said, "What a way to get out of practice—by telling them your brother died." That broke up the players. They laughed uproariously. Then Wayne Cashman took a card out of his wallet and threw it on the floor near Cheevers. "I won't need this any more," said Cashman. The goalie picked it up and started to roll on the floor with laughter. It had been McKenzie's brother's business card.

"I wonder if I could of got out of this practice if I told them my old lady had died," wondered Cheevers, and more players broke up.

When McKenzie rejoined the club, Sanderson told him, "Look at it this way, Pie. Better him than you. Who would Freddie Stanfield have on the right side if you kicked off?"

"Pie needed that," Derek was to explain later. "It took his mind off things. He cracked up when I said that."

Anyway, McKenzie had been doing that sort of thing for years to other Bruins, things so "disgusting" that even Derek wouldn't want to repeat them. A tamer episode would go like this: McKenzie would walk into the dressing room before a practice and say to Cheevers, "Gee, I'm sorry to hear about your aunt dying. You go home, I'll take care of your equipment." Or McKenzie and Cashman and Bailey and Cheevers would get into long conversations about each other's wives and children and the rest of the family, each one trying to outdo the other with outrageous stories of painful death.

The pre-game warmup was over and number 27

and his teammates left the ice. Ken Hodge was last. He always is. But once—just once—Sanderson played a trick on Hodge. He knew that after the warm-up, after each period, and after the game Hodge had to be the last one off the ice. That's just the way things were. This particular time, though, after the Bruins had won at Boston, Derek hid behind the goalie cage. Hodge made his perfunctory check, saw that everyone was off, and started to walk out. Then he heard people laughing. He looked around and saw Derek crouching behind the net. He stormed over to Derek, who was laughing insanely, grabbed him, and pushed him past the doors leading to the ice. Then Hodge stepped off.

Derek wasn't about to mess around with Hodge in his first game back, though. He let everyone do what they had always done.

On the ice, Derek's worst fears were realized. He lost three of his first four face-offs the few times he was out there killing penalties. He was nervous and he knew it. The face-offs seemed to come at critical times, too. But the Bruins won. He had played a few minutes and his shortcomings were overlooked.

Later, in the dressing room, he remembered what Orr had told him. "If the writers ask you about the game tell them about a goal. Tell them how you set up an assist. But don't get into the morals of why you would fight with someone. Don't talk about management. Just talk about the game."

Many of the players were peeved with the Boston press. The club had been going badly in Johnson's last few weeks and the old anger against newsmen had flared up again. Perhaps it had existed during the past 2½ years. Perhaps not. There hadn't been much to criticize on the Bruins in recent seasons. The club had done everything anyone could expect. Now it was losing, though, and some of the players believed the writers had unsheathed their knives and were sticking it to the players while they were down. A bunch of guys who would joke about one another's relatives dying was suddenly upset because reporters pointed out that they weren't winning.

Some of the players resolved they wouldn't talk to anyone from "the media" again. Esposito threatened to tear apart a certain writer if he appeared in the dressing room. Television sports broadcasters were being criticized and the players genuinely believed that bad things were being written because "the press has to have something to write."

"We discuss every writer, every guy on TV and radio," relates Derek. "Look, we knew when we played bush. But we didn't want it shoved down our throats. You do good things for years and then you have a few bad games and everyone's an expert and they single out certain guys. Well, the press just doesn't know what goes on inside a team, but they've got to write stories anyway. Look at Montreal. Six daily papers. For five months the Canadiens are the only team in town. Do you know how deep inside a team, into a guy, the writers have to go to be able to write six different stories a day, every day? I don't know how the guys in Montreal can take that kind of pressure. Some of them crack under it. The club loses ten games over a whole season, and each time they lose there's a dozen reasons, guys not doing their jobs, fault-finding. There's always got to be a reason, thinks the press, why a club loses, someone's to blame. And that's why players get angry. I know that John Bucyk has been playing for years with a bad back and he never mentioned it. But if John had some bad games—boom, he was suddenly too old, or he wasn't trying. Cashman had been having back problems, too. You could just sense on the bench the pain he was going through. He'd be awful quiet, and after the game he'd just dress and wince and I'd ask if the back's bothering him and he'd say, 'Yeah, a little.' But then we'd read that Cash was dogging it, that he wasn't a team guy, that he was a prima donna. Stuff like that."

All was soon forgiven. Perhaps it was the coaching change, perhaps the Bruins simply were due, perhaps Sanderson had a little something to do with it, perhaps the old pride returned—whatever the reason, the Bruins began streaking. The next night they defeated the Kings and Sanderson got his first point, an assist. A few days later he set up a short-handed goal by Sheppard and five days later he got a short-handed goal against Chicago. The Bruins were on their way and reeled off nine straight victories.

Six weeks after Derek returned Weston Adams, Sr., died.

"Derek came to the funeral with Hap Emms, which struck me as sort of strange," relates Jack Nicholson, the executive assistant to Weston Adams, Jr. "I hadn't seen the two of them together since Derek had been in the juniors."

Derek sat in the church for about five minutes, and then went out for a smoke. "I can't sit in a church," he told Nicholson. "It makes me nervous."

Sanderson also attended with Woolf. Derek turned to his lawyer and said, "I'm glad I saw the old guy in the hospital. I think I did the right thing."

The season was drawing to a close. It was by far the zaniest season on ice, when the game had changed in a way never believed possible. Certainly, it would never be the same again.

Derek, though, felt like an outsider. He was on a vague fourth line and he would kill penalties. Shakey Walton was returning off an injury and had to be worked into the line-up. There was no way that Derek would be considered ahead of Walton, who hadn't jumped the club and had stuck with it. Walton had been having a top season. He was a proven quantity, after all. Derek kept his mouth shut, followed orders, and killed penalties.

The Bruins closed with a rush and grabbed second place from the Rangers. Derek, despite part-time duty, the injuries, his condition, played in every game. In the twenty-five contests he scored five goals (two short-handed) and added ten assists. It came to a grand total of fifteen points.

Derek's longest season was to end in another week. The Bruins faced the Rangers in the first round of Stanley Cup play. It was more of the same in the opener, as far as Derek's play was concerned. He had the odd shift. Later, with the Rangers leading by 6-1 Guidolin put in Sanderson again. He scored.

The second game was another Bruin defeat, but even worse, Esposito was seriously hurt. The big man, who had never missed a Bruin game because of anything serious, was knocked out of the playoffs when he was rammed in the knee. Two teammates carried him off. Derek knew that meant he would get his chance in the next game at New York.

The last words Mr. Adams had said to Derek were, "Go show the people what kind of player you are." Now Derek was about to play in New York. He had dreams about "a Cinderella story, how I would lead the club back after two straight defeats and we'd go on and win the Stanley Cup."

Before the game in the Garden he said to himself: "Okay, now I'm going to have to do what I've been trained to do."

For one night it returned. He was in Esposito's spot, between Hodge and Cashman, centering the number 1 line. Oh, it was a little different maybe. The crowd didn't have the venom for him that it usually prepared. There was even a grudging admiration. Suddenly Derek was the focal point again, and he didn't disappoint. He was killing a penalty early in the game and stole the puck. He spotted Sheppard streaking toward center ice, fed him, and Sheppard went in to score the short-handed goal. The Bruins won the game, 4-2, and Derek had starred. There had even been a fight, his first since his return.

"Get mean," some of the guys had been telling him. "Why don't you fight?"

"How can I," he had answered, "if nobody's bothering me?"

But, he admitted later, "I was worried about getting in a fight and losing. I didn't know whether I still had the reflexes."

The man he returned to the wars against was Hadfield, the Rangers' most famous brawler. When Hadfield fights, he smashes wildly, out of control. And he is strong. He outweighs Derek by thirty-five pounds. He had recently returned, though, following a concussion. In addition, he had two bad thumbs and a broken pinky.

"I knew he had the concussion," relates Derek. Sanderson knocked Hadfield down easily. Then he straddled him. "I first hit him three overhand rights. Then I hit him twice in the back of the head while he was down."

Derek won the fight, of course. The Garden was too stunned even to boo him, although he had decked one of their heroes.

Three days later it was all over. The Bruins were knocked out of the playoffs. But Derek felt at home. He explains:

"It was like I never left, like Philadelphia was just a long road trip."